★ ☆ ★ ☆ ★ ☆ ★ ☆ ★ ☆ ★ ☆ ★

HARRY S. TRUMAN

HARRY S. TRUMAN

Barbara Silberdick Feinberg

An Impact Biography
FRANKLIN WATTS
New York   Chicago   London   Toronto   Sydney

*For my son Doug
who was born on May 8, 1972,
eighty-eight years after his hero,
President Harry S. Truman*

Memoirs by Harry S. Truman, published by Doubleday & Co., Inc., 1955, used by permission of Margaret Truman Daniel.

Excerpts from *Harry S. Truman*, by Margaret Truman, published by William Morrow & Co., Inc., 1973, used by permission of William Morrow & Co., Inc.

Photographs copyright ©: UPI/Bettmann Newsphotos: frontis, pp. 12 bottom, 13 bottom, 15, 16 top; The Harry S. Truman Library, Independence, Mo.: pp. 1, 2 bottom, 3, 4, 5 top, 6, 7 top (Office of War Information), 7 bottom (National Park Service/Abbie Rowe), 8 (U.S. Army), 9 top (U.S. Air Force), 12 top, 16 bottom; Wide World Photos: pp. 2 top, 10 top, 11, 13 top; The Kansas City Star Co.: p.5 bottom; Archive Photos, NYC: pp. 9 bottom, 14 bottom (Walter Daran); The Bettmann Archive: pp. 10 bottom, 14 top.

Library of Congress Cataloging-in-Publication Data
Feinberg, Barbara Silberdick.
Harry S. Truman / Barbara Silberdick Feinberg.
p.   cm.—(An Impact biography)
Includes bibliographical references and index.
ISBN 0-531-13036-3
1. Truman, Harry S., 1884–1972—Juvenile literature.
2. Presidents—United States—Biography—Juvenile literature.
3. United States—Politics and government—1945–1953—Juvenile literature.   [1. Truman, Harry S., 1884–1972.   2. Presidents.]
I. Title.
E814.F45   1994
973.918'092—dc20   93-30895 CIP AC
[B]

ACKNOWLEDGMENTS

I am grateful to my son Jeremy Feinberg for sharing the results of his research on the 1948 presidential election with me. I would also like to pay tribute to my late husband, Gerald Feinberg, for encouraging me through all the research and most of the revisions. I have enjoyed working with Victoria Mathews and Lorna Greenberg on this book. I have the greatest admiration for their editorial skills and professional judgment.

CONTENTS

ONE

A TIME TO
BEGIN

After spending a dreary afternoon in the Senate, Vice President Harry S. Truman was relieved when the legislature finally adjourned. He sauntered over to the private office of his friend, Speaker of the House of Representatives Sam Rayburn, who had invited him to drop by for an informal chat and a drink. Shortly after welcoming his visitor, Rayburn casually mentioned that Steve Early, President Franklin D. Roosevelt's press secretary, had phoned from the White House, asking the Vice President to get in touch with him. Truman returned the call and heard the harried press secretary say, "Please come over here as quickly and as quietly as you can."[1]

Truman immediately returned to his own office, using the underground passages in the Capitol to avoid the inevitable delays occasioned by friendly lawmakers, gawking tourists, and curious reporters. He grabbed his hat and managed to tell one of his secretaries where he was going. In his haste, he forgot to notify the Secret Service of his destination. Even though they were assigned to protect him, they usually did not follow his every move.

His black, chauffeur-driven limousine deposited him at the White House. He had no idea why he had been asked to come to the presidential mansion until he was escorted to Eleanor Roosevelt's study and saw the expression on her face. She greeted the Vice President by putting her hand on his shoulder and telling him, "Harry, the President is dead." When Truman responded, "Is there anything I can do for you?" she answered, "Is there anything we can do for *you*? You're the one in trouble now."[2]

An hour earlier President Roosevelt had died suddenly of a stroke at his vacation cottage in Warm Springs, Georgia. He had been posing for a portrait when he complained of a severe headache and lost consciousness. Within minutes he was dead. Only three months before this, on January 20, he had been sworn in to serve an unprecedented fourth term in office with a new, untried Vice President. No other president in American history had been elected to the nation's highest office so many times.

Minutes after offering Mrs. Roosevelt his sympathy and assistance, Harry Truman had to put his grief aside and make arrangements for his unexpected inauguration. During the next hour he summoned to the White House the heads of government departments, who made up the president's cabinet, congressional leaders, and the chief justice of the Supreme Court. From the President's office in the West Wing, Truman phoned his wife and daughter and broke the tragic news to them.

On Thursday evening, April 12, 1945, less than two hours after Roosevelt had died, the most powerful officials of the United States government, stunned and saddened by the news of Roosevelt's death, filed into the Cabinet Room of the White House. Having recently witnessed Roosevelt's inauguration, the solemn officials now watched sixty-year-old Vice President Harry S. Truman place his hand on a hastily borrowed Bible. They listened to Chief Justice Harlan F. Stone read the traditional oath of office and heard Truman promise to "faithfully execute the office of the President of the United States." Harry Truman, flanked by his wife and daughter, became the thirty-third President of the United States.

Those present at the swearing-in ceremony stared at

their new President, a somber man wearing round steel-rimmed glasses, a gray suit, and a blue polka-dot tie.

Silently they compared him to the smiling, confident president they mourned, wondering whether he could measure up to the job. Like previous presidents, Roosevelt had ignored his vice presidents and had given them little to do. Although Harry Truman was asked to attend the President's cabinet meetings, Roosevelt did not bring up important matters there. Even during their two private talks, the President did not choose to confide in his Vice President, preferring to share his plans for the future with only a few trusted officials and White House advisers, his "inner circle."

Although the United States was seeking to bring an end to World War II, Truman had never been briefed on the secret military plans that were expected to guarantee an Allied victory. Since 1941 the United States, Great Britain, the Soviet Union, and the other Allies had been struggling against the Axis powers—Germany, Italy, and Japan. By 1945 the Allies were winning the war, but the fighting continued. Without direct knowledge of what Roosevelt had intended to do, the new President would have to make many important decisions on his own. Roosevelt had also neglected to brief Truman about the mutual suspicions that made it difficult for the United States and Great Britain to cooperate with the Soviet Union. He had not told his Vice President about the compromises he had made with the Allies in order to establish a new international organization, the United Nations (UN), and to guarantee the security of the postwar world.

Many of the officials assembled in the Cabinet Room for Truman's hasty inauguration supposed that this untested and poorly prepared Vice President would simply depend on them to carry out Roosevelt's wishes. They expected Truman to take their advice without question and merely to serve as a caretaker for the Roosevelt administration. However, they quickly found out that they had underestimated their new President. Immediately after being sworn in, Truman called a meeting of the cabinet and took control of the proceedings. As he was taking his seat at the head of the table, the presidential press secretary came in with an urgent question from newspaper reporters. They wanted to know if President Truman intended to go ahead with the San Francisco conference to draft the UN Charter, planned for April 25. The charter would establish the fundamental structure and procedures of the organization. Without consulting the assembled department heads, Truman immediately announced that the conference would be held as scheduled.

By taking this action, the new President made it clear that he and he alone was in charge of the government. During the meeting that followed, he also did most of the talking. After urging Roosevelt's cabinet appointees to stay at their posts, Truman laid down the ground rules he expected these experienced administrators to follow: "I was President, and they could . . . tell me if they thought I was wrong, but in the long run, I said . . . I'd make the final decisions, and I'd expect them to support me."[3] He was determined to make his own place in history, not to follow meekly in Roosevelt's footsteps, guided by the late president's advisers.

From 1945 to 1953, Truman made many important decisions that would shape the next forty years of American history and beyond. In foreign policy, he chose to hasten the conclusion of World War II by using atomic bombs to defeat Japan. He spearheaded the drive to reorganize American defense institutions and to rebuild Western Europe in order to resist Soviet expansion in Europe and Asia. On the domestic front, he took the first steps toward integrating blacks and whites in the United States military, tried to protect government employees from congressional scrutiny of their loyalty, and smoothed the transition between incoming and outgoing government administrations. His was indeed a remarkable legacy for future generations of Americans.

By an odd coincidence, Harry Truman was related to John Tyler, the first vice president to become chief executive upon the death of a president. Tyler assumed his new responsibilities in April 1841, when President William Henry Harrison died of pneumonia shortly after being sworn in. Other members of the Truman family were not to be found in the pages of history books because they were unremarkable hard-working people who had survived the rigors of the Civil War without fanfare or fuss. One of Harry Truman's grandfathers, Anderson Shippe Truman, was a Missouri farmer. Although his other grandfather, Solomon Young, owned a large farm, he led a more adventurous life, guiding wagon trains from Missouri to California and Utah between 1840 and 1870 and supplying pioneers with the equipment they needed.

Truman's parents, John Anderson Truman and Martha Ellen Young, were married in 1881. Martha, educated at the Baptist Female College in Lexington, Missouri, was a well-informed and opinionated pioneer woman. Years later, when her famous son invited her to stay at the White House, she refused to sleep in the Lincoln bedroom because she had never forgiven the Yankees for looting the family farm during the Civil War. Less well educated than his wife, John turned to farming, horse trading, and speculating in grain. He was not very successful, but he somehow managed to provide for his small family.

Harry S. Truman was born on May 8, 1884, in Lamar, Missouri, where his parents owned a small farm. He was named for his uncle Harrison Young, with the initial S replacing the customary middle name because his parents did not wish to offend either of his grandfathers by choosing between Shippe and Solomon. In 1886 his parents presented him with a brother, John Vivian, named for a Confederate cavalry officer; the younger Truman preferred to be known by his middle name, Vivian. The family was completed in 1889 with the birth of Harry's sister, given the name Mary Jane in memory of John Truman's mother. The three children were to remain close for the rest of their lives. Harry was three years old when the Truman family moved to the 600-acre Young farm, in Grandview, Missouri. Like most farm children, from a very early age he was trained to make himself useful and was expected to perform simple chores like feeding the chickens. However, work had its rewards—rides on a Shetland pony and trips to the fair with his Grandfather Young, whom he adored.

Gradually, Martha Truman began to notice that Harry had trouble seeing distant objects even though he had little difficulty learning to read from the large-print family Bible. When he was six years old, she took him to an eye doctor in nearby Kansas City, who prescribed eyeglasses for him. In the 1890s, it was uncommon for children to have their eyes examined and to wear glasses, so Harry Truman became an object of curiosity and occasional teasing. As he explained, "Of course, they called me *four-eyes* and a lot of other things, too. That's hard on a boy. It makes him lonely."[4] Because his eyeglasses could easily be broken, he wasn't able to play baseball, roughhouse, or participate in other activities most children enjoyed. So it was no wonder that Harry struck people as a bit of a sissy, a mama's boy. It did not help that he was a polite, agreeable youngster who spent a lot of time at home helping his mother care for his baby sister.

Unable to join the other boys in their wilder games, and uncomfortable around them, Harry nevertheless found ways to amuse himself. He spent most of his free time absorbed in books about great people and events of the past. This was a natural choice for a boy who grew up on Martha Truman's tales of the Civil War and how the Yankees had stolen her family's silver and feather beds. She bought him Horne's *Great Men and Famous Women*, which led him to develop a lifelong fondness for biographies and histories. Later, his interest in ancient history even led him and a friend to build a model of a wooden bridge Julius Caesar had used to cross the Rhine.

In 1890, Martha Truman encouraged John to use a

legacy from his father to move the family to Independence, Missouri, where many Truman relatives lived. She wanted her children to have a better education than was available to them in Grandview. Independence, a small town of about 6,000 inhabitants, contained two bookstores and a library as well as good schools. In this midwestern community, neighbors helped each other out, nursing the sick or simply borrowing a cup of sugar. They trusted each other as well, conducting many business deals with a shake of the hand rather than a legal agreement. These were people who read the newspapers and enjoyed discussing what went on in the rest of the nation. At the turn of the century, before the advent of radio, television, and movies, people amused themselves by going to picnics, hayrides, and parties.

During Harry's childhood, Independence still bore traces of its ties to the Confederacy and its frontier past. Although the people were farmers rather than plantation owners, many of them had been slaveholders before the Civil War, and they regarded the free blacks as unwelcome inferiors, barring them from patronizing local stores and the library. Citizens remembered and romanticized raiders like William Quantrill, who massacred Union sympathizers in Kansas from hiding places on the Missouri side of the border. They also recalled stories about outlaws, including members of the Dalton gang and Jesse James, whose brother Frank had spent time in the local jail. Harry and his friends like to play in the yard, pretending they were riding with the Daltons or the James brothers. Known for his love of history, Harry was often called upon to settle arguments about how many bank robbers there were and which outlaws were killed. He had finally found companions among children his own age, who accepted him as he was—bookish, serious, and limited athletically by his need to wear eyeglasses. They respected his knowledge and even refrained from teasing him after he began to study the piano, at that time a pursuit usually reserved for girls.

The family fortunes gradually improved after their

arrival in Independence, and the Trumans were able to purchase a piano when Harry was eleven. Believing that her son had some talent, Martha Truman found a music teacher for him. He took lessons seriously and did not mind practicing two hours a day while other boys his age were outside playing and getting into mischief. When he had learned all he could from his local teacher, he agreed to work with an instructor in Kansas City, who had been trained by some of the outstanding American and European pianists of the day. His music meant so much to him that he was even willing to take a twice a week ten-mile trip on the streetcar to study with her. Instead of playing the popular songs of the day, he studied classical music, including the works of Chopin and Mozart, which he particularly enjoyed. He did not give up his lessons until he was seventeen years old; he continued to play the piano for the rest of his life.

When he was fourteen, Harry worked for a brief time in a drugstore, mopping floors, washing bottles, and tidying up from six-thirty in the morning until it was time to go to school. On weekends he worked from four in the afternoon until ten at night, all for the princely sum of three dollars a week. He not only learned the value of hard work but also developed a reputation as a dependable and responsible young man. However, after three months of these tedious chores, his father insisted that he leave the job to spend more time on his high school studies.

Harry Truman was a good student, but he was not the smartest boy in his class. Top honors went to his friend Charlie Ross, who later became a newspaperman and would eventually become Truman's presidential press secretary. Friends rather than competitors, the two boys started a school magazine, *The Gleam*. Since they were both fond of Latin, they also worked together preparing their own translation of selections from Cicero's works. Harry also went over the Latin assignments with his cousins Ethel and Nellie Noland, his closest friends. Classmate

Bess Wallace would sometimes study with them. Harry had known and admired Bess Wallace since he first saw her in Sunday school, but he always felt tongue-tied and awkward around her. Unlike Harry, she was an excellent athlete and came from one of the town's leading families. The Nolands made it easier for Harry to get to know the girl he adored.

While Harry's mother had introduced him to books and music, his father helped to develop his interest in politics. At age sixteen Harry joined his father at the 1900 Democratic National Convention in Kansas City. While running errands for local politicians, he found time to listen to the stirring oratory of presidential candidate William Jennings Bryan, who spoke vividly against people with great wealth and power. Bryan's speeches defending the interests of the average citizen may have struck a responsive chord in the young Truman, for they charted the direction his life would take. Post–Civil War Independence was a Democratic stronghold, so it was no surprise that Harry Truman soon joined the party and became a lifelong member.

His high school years marked the end of Harry Truman's formal education, making him the last American President who was not a college graduate. Throughout Truman's life, his father's income had suffered periodic ups and downs, and when Harry was ready to go to college, his father could not afford to pay the tuition. Saddled with debts from his speculations in grain, John Truman had to move back to the Young family farm in Grandview. Harry had thought about applying to the U.S. Military Academy to continue his education at the government's expense. In the hope of preparing himself for admission to West Point, he had put in extra time on his studies, but his poor eyesight disqualified him from passing the academy's physical examination. Instead, he worked as a timekeeper for the Santa Fe Railroad, where he gained experience in handling men much older, rowdier, and stronger than he was. For the sum of $35 a month and board, he recorded the hours railroad work gangs put in and managed the weekly payroll.

Harry would always regard Independence as his hometown, but in 1904 he moved on to Kansas City, Missouri, and took a job as a bank clerk and a part-time theater usher. While guiding people to their seats in the theater, he managed to see some of the traveling variety shows that featured the top stars of the day. He soon won promotions at the bank and began to earn as much as $120 a month, a pretty good sum in those days. Yet in 1906, when his father asked him to come home to help manage the Young family farm, Harry Truman immediately resigned from the bank and returned to Grandview, Missouri. Whatever his own aspirations may have been, his father's needs came first.

As a child Harry had done simple farm chores, but now he was called upon to do a man's work. Farming in the early 1900s required much physical strength and stamina, since the men tended the fields without the benefit of tractors and other labor-saving machinery. They milked the cows by hand and used horses or mules for plowing. Harry had to learn to plow a straight furrow. As he said once, "If it wasn't, I heard about it from my father for the next year."[5] John Truman was not only a hard worker but a perfectionist as well. Given the demands on his body, it is no wonder that five-foot, ten-inch Harry Truman developed a sturdy muscular build as he worked on the land. By 1911, Harry's brother, Vivian, had married and left the Young farm to run a place of his own. At that point, John Truman made Harry a full partner in the farm, which also meant that the son had to assume full responsibility for his father's debts.

Although farming was a demanding occupation, Harry found time to learn about local politics. On Election Day he served as Democratic clerk, keeping count of the ballots while getting to know most of the voters in the area. In addition, he assisted his father when John Truman became road overseer, a minor political post requiring him to supervise the repair and upkeep of the township roads, a time-consuming and unrewarding task. Although the pay was meager and the work never-ending, John volunteered to take on this unpopular job because he enjoyed any kind of political task, no matter how menial. Both father and son earned the township's respect by greatly improving road maintenance in the area and by showing that any job, even a disagreeable one, could be done well.

Harry also managed to resume his friendship with Bess Wallace, even though he had to depend on unreliable train schedules and complicated streetcar routes to travel the sixteen miles to Independence to see her. His Noland cousins, now teachers, lived on the same street as Bess and often invited him to sleep over on a sofa in their parlor, sparing him a two-hour return trip. During the days they were apart, Harry and Bess wrote to each other frequently. Although Harry's skill at spelling left something to be desired, he found it much easier to tell Bess how he felt about her in letters than to talk with her in person. However, most of his letters to her contained straightforward accounts of his daily life on the farm and his opinions about literature, politics, religion, and whatever else interested him at the time.

Over her mother's objections, Bess welcomed visits from Harry Truman, for she respected the hardworking, studious farmer she had known most of her life. Unlike her mother, Madge Wallace, who thought no one was good enough to marry her daughter, Bess judged people by their character, not their social position. To her mother's great relief, however, Bess was in no hurry to marry and would continue to look after her. Since 1909, when her father died, Bess had been the head of the Wallace family, taking charge of her dependent widowed mother and three younger brothers, and like Harry, she took her responsibilities seriously. Perhaps this is why she turned down his first offer of marriage in 1911, but in 1913, to Harry's great surprise, Bess finally agreed to a secret engagement. However, the couple did not make any plans for an immediate marriage. This was just as well because in November 1914, John Truman died, leaving Harry to pay off his debts, run the family farm, and care for his mother and sister. Harry calmly accepted these added responsibilities while Bess continued to manage the Wallace family affairs.

In 1917 the United States entered World War I, siding with British and French troops who had been fighting the imperial armies of Germany and Austria since 1914. Caught up in the patriotic fervor, Harry Truman volunteered to serve in the army. He could easily have remained at home if he had chosen to claim exemption as a farmer contributing to the war effort or as the sole support of his widowed mother and his sister. Since he was physically disabled by poor eyesight and older than the maximum draft age, it was something short of a miracle that he convinced the military to take him. Bess pleaded with him to marry her right away, but Truman refused, explaining in a letter, "Bess, I'm dead crazy to ask you to marry me before I leave but I'm not going to do it because I don't think it would be right for me to ask you to tie yourself to a prospective cripple."[6] He knew that World War I had already produced a great number of casualties, and he was aware of the fact that he might become one of these statistics.

Harry Truman had joined the National Guard when he lived in Kansas City. Because of this, when he signed up, he was made a lieutenant in charge of an artillery outfit and was sent for training to an encampment near Fort Sill, Oklahoma. Aside from his military duties, he ran the regimental canteen with the help of an enlisted man, Eddie Jacobson. The canteen sold candy, cigarettes, and stationery to the recruits and even showed a profit, something most canteens failed to do. Once his training was completed, Truman was supplied with three extra pairs of glasses and shipped off to France.

He was placed in command of Battery D of the 129th

Field Artillery, made up of unruly soldiers who had managed to get rid of three previous commanding officers. His experience working with railroad work gangs helped him whip the men into a fighting unit and win their respect. Although he was a strict disciplinarian, he did not just bark out orders and walk away; he got to know all of his men personally, saw to their well-being, and earned their loyalty. Sent to the Vosges Mountains for combat experience, Truman and his green troops fought what they later called the Battle of Who Run. As Truman described it, the sector had been very quiet until the Germans started firing, panicking an American sergeant, who yelled that all of the men should run for their lives. Truman expected more from Battery D. "I stood right there," he said, "and I called them every name I could think of, which was plenty, and they came sneaking back and got the horses and the battery in a position of safety."[7] Promoted to captain, Truman went on to see action in one of the major battles of World War I, the Argonne Forest. Under fire, and with little regard for his own safety, he directed his artillerymen to shell the enemy. None of the men who served under him would ever forget his blunt language or his bravery, nor would they forget that amid all the carnage, only one man from Battery D was killed, and only two were wounded.

At the war's end, despite his interest in history, Truman paid little attention to the peace settlement being negotiated in Paris. Like many American soldiers, all he wanted to do was go home. As he wrote to his cousin Ethel Noland, "Most of us don't give a whoop (to put it mildly) whether Russia has a Red Government or no Government and if the King of the Lollypops wants to slaughter his subjects or his Prime Minister it's all the same to us."[8] However, he and his men had to wait from November 1918, when the Armistice was declared, until April 1919 before they were finally shipped home. By then he and Bess had already exchanged letters outlining plans for their wedding.

Harry Truman married Bess Wallace on June 28,

1919, in a church wedding, which was followed by an outdoor reception at the Wallace home. After a brief honeymoon in Chicago and Port Huron, Michigan, the thirty-five-year-old couple returned to Independence to live with Bess's mother. The arrangement was convenient for both the bride and the groom, since Harry was just beginning a new career and had little money to support a wife, and Bess was not eager to leave the Wallace household where she had strong, loving ties to her family and still felt responsible for her mother's welfare. Despite her continuing disapproval of Harry Truman, Mrs. Wallace was willing to house the newlyweds because she could not bear to be separated from her daughter. Despite his mother-in-law's constant criticism of him, Harry Truman treated her with courtesy and respect and gradually came to think of her house at 219 North Delaware Street as home. Over the years he grew quite fond of the fourteen-room white clapboard dwelling with its spacious porches and large lawn.

Having given up farming, Truman opened up a haberdashery—a men's clothing store—in Kansas City in partnership with Eddie Jacobson, the man who had helped him run the wartime regimental canteen. The two men got off to a good start, attracting customers from among the local men who had served in Battery D. In 1921, however, the economy slowed down, producing a sharp drop in farm prices. This left small businesses in farming communities with few customers able to purchase their goods—in Truman's case, to buy new shirts and ties. In fact, Truman's army buddies appealed to him for loans, much as they had during the war. He tried to help them out, but with a large unsold inventory of men's furnishings, he and his partner were facing financial ruin. In 1922 the haberdashery was forced to close when sales continued to decline. Jacobson eventually went into bankruptcy, while Truman gradually managed to pay off his debts.

During the first four decades of his life, Harry Truman had learned how to deal with physical handicaps and personal disappointments and was able to make his own way in the world. While working with railroad crews and an artillery unit, he found he had an ability to handle men, and he had developed firsthand an understanding of the troubles farmers and small businessmen faced. The values of small-town America were his values: hard work, self-discipline, optimism, and a faith in humanity. If the opportunity arose, given his background and experiences, he would be a most attractive candidate for political office.

A CAREER IN POLITICS

In Oak Grove, Missouri, farmers from all over Jackson County gathered for the grandest political picnic of the summer of 1922. They looked forward to listening to the local candidates give speeches, for they regarded politics as a form of entertainment as well as enlightenment. As they sat on the grass chatting, they noticed an airplane, an old Spinning Jenny left over from World War I, hovering above them. The plane slowly circled the picnic grounds, dropping leaflets on the assembled farmers asking them to vote for Harry S. Truman, a candidate for a local government post. This was the first time the Missouri farmers had been bombarded from the air with requests for their support; however, their attention was soon diverted from the falling leaflets.

After the plane landed in a nearby pasture, they watched with horror as it continued to roll on and on while the pilot desperately tried to get it to stop. The anxious farmers thought it would certainly crash into the surrounding barbed-wire fence. The engine spluttered, and the plane finally came to a halt just three feet from the fence. Out of the cockpit climbed the pilot, along with candidate Truman, looking the worse for his experience. He slowly walked to the platform and gave his campaign speech in his usual flat, high-pitched voice.

Just before his haberdashery was forced to close,

Harry Truman had agreed to become a candidate for local office. He was asked to run for county commissioner of public works, a position that carried the misleading title of "county judge" in Missouri. The Missouri county court was actually a commission that issued contracts to have roads paved, arranged to erect public buildings at the taxpayers' expense, and hired overseers to supervise these construction projects. Jim Pendergast, who had served with Truman in the 129th Infantry, had urged him to seek election as a county judge and had offered him the support of the Pendergast family. From their base in Kansas City, Boss Tom Pendergast and his family controlled much of western Missouri politics through a political machine they had organized. Political machines, common in many parts of the United States at that time, chose candidates for nomination and election, brought out the vote, and awarded favors, including lucrative contracts for public projects, to faithful party members. They also appointed loyal supporters to government jobs, a practice known as political patronage.

For years, members of the Jackson County Democratic party had fought among themselves for control of political posts and had finally divided into two factions. These were the Pendergast machine, known as the Goats, and the Shannon machine, called the Rabbits, odd names that probably arose because the original Pendergast supporters kept goats while the Shannon people lived in a rabbit-infested area.[1] Because the Republican party in Jackson County was so weak that it offered little competition at the polls, the August primary elections for nominations among Democratic factions were more hotly contested than the November elections between Republican and Democratic candidates. In 1922 five Rabbit and Goat candidates would be competing to win nominations for three posts as county judges.

Harry Truman was well aware of the role machines played in politics, but he accepted the Pendergasts' offer;

he knew it would be difficult to win an election in Jackson County without their backing. On his own, however, he gained the support of the county's farmers who knew him from Grandview, World War I veterans who had served with him, and his many Truman relatives who lived in Jackson County. Nevertheless, his introduction to politicking was far from smooth. As he recalled, "My first speech was out at the town of Lee's Summit . . . and I was so scared I couldn't say a word. So I just got off the platform."[2] He campaigned by driving an old Dodge roadster to each of the seven townships that made up Jackson County, making speeches wherever he could find an audience. He spoke bluntly about himself and did not hide the fact that his business had failed. "Most people were broke," he said later, "and they sympathized with a man in politics who admitted his financial condition."[3] When the ballots were cast on August 1, Truman won by a margin of 300 votes. His primary victory virtually guaranteed his election for a two-year term.

Once in office, Judge Truman did not always behave like a typical Jackson County politician, nor did his colleague Judge Henry McElroy. Instead of spending money on needless projects to demonstrate their own importance to the community, the two men did their best to reduce the county debt run up by their predecessors. Furthermore, they turned down bribes to award road contracts to construction firms with a reputation for shoddy materials and poor workmanship, even though these firms had previously done business with the county. On the other hand, as judges with county jobs to distribute, Truman and McElroy showed their loyalty to the Goats by awarding patronage posts only to members of their own party faction. Of course, by excluding the Shannon faction from the county payroll, the two judges made some powerful enemies who were determined to get even with them at the next election.

In the fall of 1922, Truman faced a more dangerous

foe, the Ku Klux Klan, which had attracted a large following during the 1920s with its message of hatred toward blacks, Jews, "foreigners," and Catholics. Truman was introduced to a Klan organizer who wanted him to promise that he would not give county jobs to Catholics, even though Truman's backers, the Pendergasts, were Catholics. Truman replied, "I had a Catholic battery in the war, and if any of those boys need help, I'm going to give them a job."[4] The Shannon Rabbits and the Ku Klux Klan threw their support to the Republican candidate, and in 1924, Harry Truman was defeated in an election for the first and only time in his life, losing by 877 votes.

He had cause for celebration on February 17, 1924, however, when Bess gave birth to their daughter, Margaret. To support them, Truman took a variety of jobs, including an assignment to recruit members for the Kansas City Automobile Club. He also became president of the National Old Trails Association, marking historic roads and sites, and served as vice president of a savings and loan association. For two years he had been taking law courses, but now they failed to hold his interest, and he abandoned his studies. Unlike most of his contemporaries, he was oblivious to the Roaring Twenties. He did not spend his free time listening to jazz, dancing the Charleston, playing bridge and golf, or reading novels about the "lost generation." All he wanted to do was to get back into politics.

That opportunity came when the Pendergasts urged Truman to run for presiding judge, or chief commissioner, of the county court in the 1926 elections. After two years of Republican rule, the Democratic Goats and Rabbits had joined forces to defeat their common Republican enemy. Truman began his first four-year term by winning with a 16,000 vote margin, and in 1930 he was reelected by 58,000 votes. In this post, Truman was in charge of 700 county employees, a $7 million budget, two courthouses and their jails, a home for the aged, three orphanages, a hospital, and thousands of miles of roads. He relished these responsibilities. The new presiding judge was determined to put county public works on a sound and honest financial basis. In the past, the county had borrowed funds from local banks at 6½ percent interest; Truman saved the taxpayers money by negotiating loans at 4 percent and, later, at 2½ percent interest. Finally he persuaded Jackson County voters to accept two bond issues as a means of raising the money for needed improvements.

Truman developed a reputation for honesty and fairness in spending these funds. He personally inspected the 225 miles of roads that had been paved as a result of his programs. He visited a number of county courthouses in the United States before settling on a design for the courthouse in Kansas City and took great pride in its construction, which he closely supervised. He also had the Independence courthouse renovated. He was under enormous pressure from old acquaintances, contractors, and the Pendergast machine to divert public monies into their pockets, as his predecessors had done. Describing the situation, he commented: "The county was in debt when I got in because the previous occupants of the job were the kind who were always standing with their hands out when contracts were let for buildings or roads or anything at all. I put a stop to it, and I came out of the county courts after ten years of service a damn sight worse off than when I went into it."[5]

He developed severe headaches and insomnia, probably because he stood his ground. When the Pendergasts criticized him for failing to grant contracts to their friends, he defended his right to select companies that would do the best work at the lowest cost. He even hired out-of-state firms when they proved most efficient. He also rejected all attempts to bribe him. Truman believed very strongly in party loyalty, but he just as firmly deplored political corruption. Seeking refuge from the constant barrage of dubious requests and questionable demands, he went on trips to survey public works in other states and participated yearly in two-week summer army training camp exercises.

Truman rarely took the pressures of his job home. To Margaret, he was an indulgent father, bringing gifts home each time he was away from Independence. It was up to Bess to discipline their child.

On Sundays, Harry drove his wife and daughter to visit his mother in Grandview, where he unwound as he listened to Martha Truman's uninhibited, opinionated discussions about whatever interested her at the moment. Meals with his mother were certainly less stiff and formal than dinners at Mrs. Wallace's home. At the end of the weekly visits, Martha would often caution him, "Now, Harry, be good," or "Being too good is apt to be uninteresting."[6]

Truman was made a member of the Missouri delegation to the 1932 Democratic National Convention, the convention that first nominated Franklin Roosevelt for President. With the nation's economy at a standstill as a result of the Great Depression, some 12 million Americans were unemployed. In Independence during 1931 and 1932, about 2,800 people were getting assistance from community organizations, and many of them had to be fed at the local soup kitchen; by 1933, the number had reached 4,347.[7] Voters were hopeful when they heard about Roosevelt's promised New Deal, a program of relief that would provide help for the needy as well as public works projects to give people jobs. Later, in the aftermath of Roosevelt's overwhelming victory, Harry Truman was appointed federal reemployment director for Missouri, with the task of getting unemployed workers jobs on government-funded public works projects. He waived the pay so that he could keep his post as presiding judge.

Nineteen thirty-four was a senatorial election year in Missouri. It was important to the Pendergast machine and the politicians of rural western Missouri that their candidate get the nomination rather than someone supported by

Democratic Senator Bennett Champ Clark and the eastern Missouri–Saint Louis machine. Many New Deal patronage jobs were at stake. Tarnished by their association with a notorious Kansas City gangster, the Pendergasts needed a candidate with an unblemished record, but the men they asked to run turned them down. They finally offered Truman the nomination because of his impressive record for honesty. Truman seized the opportunity and threw himself into the primary contest with gusto.

He campaigned in sixty Missouri counties, traveling by car and making as many as sixteen speeches a day. Even an automobile accident did not prevent him from keeping up this exhausting schedule. The Saint Louis Democrats tried to smear Truman by bringing up his ties to the corrupt Pendergast machine. They also referred to the debts he owed from his failed haberdashery. The voters quickly realized that Truman's debt was proof that despite his connection with the Pendergasts, he had not taken bribes when he held county office. In August, when the primary election was held, Truman won the Democratic party nomination. In November, he defeated the Republican incumbent, Senator Roscoe Patterson, by about 250,000 votes.

In January 1935 fifty-year-old Harry Truman, his wife, and his daughter settled into a cramped four-room Washington apartment, a striking contrast to the spacious Wallace home in Missouri. Bess doubted that they could afford the $150 a month rent, given the senator's $10,000 yearly salary. During Truman's senatorial years, the family moved to a number of temporary quarters in search of reasonable rent and adequate space. For financial and family reasons, Bess and Margaret spent only half the year in Washington. During the other half of the year, they returned to Independence. Although Bess enjoyed the social life in Washington, she missed her family and friends, and had to take care of her aging mother. From her home on North Delaware Street, Bess could also keep her husband informed of the latest developments in Missouri politics. Living alone in Washington for part of each year, Truman also missed his family and friends in Independence. Dinner invitations poured in from Washington hostesses eager to have an extra man at the table, but he rarely enjoyed the lavish parties he was pressed to attend and limited his social engagements. However, the parties served a useful purpose, offering Truman opportunities to get to know the members of the Senate and learn the customs of the exclusive club he had joined.

As one of thirteen freshman senators, Harry Truman was ill at ease in his new post. The Senate was like an exclusive gentlemen's club with its own customs and traditions. For example, newcomers were expected to be seen, not heard, to work hard and not grab headlines. It wasn't clear how a blunt, outspoken farmer and failed haberdasher was going to fit in. Harry explained that at first he felt ill at ease, but then a longtime senator came over to him and said, "Harry, the first six months you're here, you'll wonder how in hell you got here, and after that, you'll wonder how the hell the rest of us got here."[8] He was right.

Following the practices he had set for himself as a county judge, Truman drove himself to measure up to his new responsibilities and soon earned his colleagues' respect. Night after night, after visiting the Library of Congress, he carried home stacks of reading material so that he could vote intelligently on the bills coming before the Senate. He was assigned to the Appropriations Committee, which funded all government programs, and to the Interstate Commerce Committee, which regulated the nation's transportation and trade. Because of his nightly studying, he gradually received recognition as an expert on government spending. Unlike many senators, he did not skip committee meetings and was rewarded for his faithful attendance by being asked to preside over a sub-committee looking into railroad corruption and mismanagement. Truman also chaired hearings on air transportation. His findings on the troubled state of aviation finances led him to sponsor a bill creating the Civil Aeronautics Authority Board and strengthening commercial aviation.

During his first term in the Senate, Democratic loyalist Harry Truman voted for most of Roosevelt's New Deal legislation, including the right of workers to bargain with employers, Social Security pensions for the elderly and handicapped, unemployment insurance, flood control, and aid to farmers. He even supported the President's controversial plan to increase the number of justices sitting on the Supreme Court when most senators did not. He knew that on several occasions in the past Congress had changed the size of the Supreme Court, so he willingly stood by his President. Historians insist that by threatening to add new members, Roosevelt was applying pressure to get the Supreme Court to accept his New Deal reforms. However, the Congress, reluctant to tamper with another branch of government, rejected the "court-packing" plan. The only time Truman openly defied Roosevelt was when he voted in favor of a bonus to veterans. Although the President opposed the bill, Truman, as a former veteran, could not disappoint the men with whom he had served in World War I. Besides, he reasoned that the veterans would spend the money rather than save it. Collectively, their spending would create a greater demand for goods and thus create jobs for the unemployed.

Martha Truman, a Roosevelt supporter, often wrote to her son, airing her views on national issues. According to him, "She read the *Congressional Record* [a daily account of what the lawmakers were saying and doing] every day, and she understood what was going on a lot better than some senators I could mention. And she was one of my constituents, in addition to being my mother, and she had every right to write to me."[9] Their correspondence, though, did not cause the independent senator to alter his own views. Away from his beloved hometown, Truman exchanged letters with other family members as well, but there is no reason to believe that his relatives exerted undue political pressure.

As the election of 1940 approached, Harry Truman returned to Independence more and more frequently once other Missouri Democrats decided to challenge him for the party's nomination. Federal District Attorney Maurice Milligan, who had made a name for himself by successfully prosecuting Tom Pendergast for bribery and failure to pay income taxes, announced that he would run for Truman's Senate seat. The popular governor of Missouri, Lloyd Stark, a friend whom Truman first brought to Pendergast's attention as a possible gubernatorial candidate, also entered the race. Roosevelt thought Truman's chances of renomination were so bleak that he offered to appoint him to the Interstate Commerce Commission, an independent agency that regulated the rates that railroads, truckers, and ships could charge for transporting goods from one state to another. However, the feisty senator from Missouri refused to give up his seat without a fight—even though he found that he would have to win the primary election for the nomination without the President's backing. Despite Truman's support for his policies, Roosevelt would not endorse any of the candidates in such an uncertain race. However, the President's neutrality was not the reason Truman decided to oppose Roosevelt's bid for a third term in office. As a student of history, Truman reasoned that it was unhealthy for democratic government to become too dependent on one person.

During the primary campaign, Truman's ties to the Pendergasts haunted him once again even though Tom Pendergast was now in prison and the machine had lost much of its power. Truman's opponents pointed out that he had opposed Milligan's reappointment as federal district attorney; they also charged that he had accepted bribes. However, Truman didn't even have the money to help his mother when her mortgage was foreclosed and she had to leave her farm, so that attempt to discredit him eventually backfired. Newspaper articles persistently questioned Truman's refusal to condemn the Pendergast machine. "I wouldn't kick a friend who was in trouble no matter what it might do to win me votes," was his indignant reply.[10] Truman would never be disloyal to his party or to his old friends—even if his loyalty cost him the election.

He courageously kicked off his campaign in Sedalia, Missouri, speaking about civil rights before a crowd that included former members of the Ku Klux Klan. Also present in Sedalia was his mother, who still bore a grudge against the North for winning the Civil War. No blacks were present when Truman stated: "I believe in the brotherhood of man, not merely the brotherhood of white men, but the brotherhood of all men before the law. . . . The majority of our Negro people find cold comfort in shanties and tenements. Surely, as freemen, they are entitled to something better than this."[11] In the Senate, he had backed legislation to end poll taxes (fees that effectively kept blacks from voting) and had supported anti-lynching bills (to prevent armed groups of white citizens from taking the law in their own hands and murdering blacks for minor offenses or imagined crimes). His commitment to civil rights for blacks continued throughout his public career.

Although Truman was considered an underdog, his voting record on New Deal laws, his support for the veterans' bonus, as well as his work in committees reforming the railroads and airlines helped him win votes among farmers, workers, veterans, and blacks. A number of senators came to Missouri to campaign for him along with Senator Bennett Clark, who turned the tide in Truman's favor by convincing the head of the Saint Louis political machine, Robert Hannegan, to shift his support to Truman. On August 5, the eve of the primary election, in what was to become a Truman family tradition, Harry Truman went to bed early, confident that he would win. His wife and daughter did not share his optimism and stayed up late, anxiously awaiting the returns. Truman won Saint Louis by eight thousand votes, just as he had expected. In November he won reelection to the Senate against Republican Manvel Davis by 44,000 votes, a smaller margin of victory than he had in 1934, but by 1940 the Republican party was regaining strength nationwide.

When Harry Truman returned to the Senate in January 1941, the lawmakers were rushing to build up American defenses, neglected since 1919, when Americans had chosen to isolate themselves from foreign affairs. Soon after the outbreak of World War II in 1939, the Axis forces had succeeded in conquering most of Europe and Asia, and by the summer of 1940 Britain faced the enemy alone. Belatedly, Congress had passed laws drafting men into the armed services, funding hastily constructed bases to house them, and authorizing contracts to spur the production of war matériel in a frantic effort to re-arm. The lawmakers were even willing to send military supplies to Britain, reversing the policy that as a neutral nation, the United States would support neither side in the conflict so as not to be drawn into another European war. Harry Truman had long been urging his senatorial colleagues to help Britain, and they finally realized that the quick military triumph of the Axis over most of Europe posed a potential threat to the United States.

In America's desperate rush to prepare for the possibility of war, mistakes were bound to be made. So Harry Truman proposed that the Senate set up a Committee to Investigate the National Defense Program, later known as Truman and his committee. For the previous twenty years he had unknowingly prepared for this job by dealing with contractors and supervising the construction of public works in Jackson County. As committee chairman, Truman insisted that witnesses be treated with courtesy, and while he was clearly in charge, he did not dominate the proceedings. With unusual objectivity and an utter lack of theatrics, Truman and his committee discovered that some of the contractors building army bases were making three or four times their yearly incomes for three-month jobs. They also found that southern coal mine owners were blocking settlement of a miners' strike.

As a result of these initial findings, the Senate voted the committee more funding to continue its scrutiny of the defense effort. This enabled Truman to hire first-rate investigators and to hold committee hearings in different parts of the country. Because the newspapers publicized the committee's carefully documented findings of waste, duplication, and fraud, people began to volunteer even more information about the misuse of federal funds. The failed small businessman and his committee were taking on some of the largest corporations in America and making them accountable to the public. As the committee's work load increased and conditions in Europe continued to deteriorate, Truman found himself experiencing severe headaches once again. Doctors at Bethesda Naval Hospital attributed the headaches to fatigue, but given the work he was doing, Truman knew the pressures would only increase.

Because Truman was so busy investigating the defense program, in 1941 his wife and daughter moved to Washington, D.C., permanently. They settled in a five-room apartment on Connecticut Avenue that would serve as their home for the next four years. Of course, Bess could no longer keep him informed about Missouri politics, but instead, she became a full-time salaried employee in her husband's office. She helped out by handling his mail, meeting with visiting Missourians, and generally running things when he was on one of his many trips around the country. Seventeen-year-old Margaret was relieved to no longer have to divide her schooling between Washington and Independence.

When the Japanese unexpectedly attacked Pearl Harbor, Hawaii, on December 7, 1941, the United States entered World War II. As the nation's economy hastily switched over from making consumer goods to making military supplies, the Truman Committee uncovered shocking evidence of inefficiency and corruption. For example, the senators proved that the army and the Curtiss-Wright company were covering up the manufacture of four hundred defective airplane engines; they also found fault with the length of the wings on the Martin B-26 bomber. During the investigations, Truman did not hesitate to question the activities of the nation's top industrial and military leaders. He did, however, reluctantly heed Secretary of War Henry Stimson's request not to look into the top-secret Manhattan Project which, unknown to Truman, was developing an atomic bomb.

In 1943 he took time out from committee investigations to give a speech in Chicago urging a safe haven for the European Jews being slaughtered by the Germans. Unlike many at the time, he did believe that the Germans were committing atrocities against the Jews, and he felt the United States government was not doing enough to help these victims of persecution. Five years later he would help Jewish survivors gain recognition for the state of Israel, their safe haven.

Once regarded as a shady politician controlled by the Pendergast machine, brisk and energetic Harry Truman had become a highly respected senator with a national reputation for his hard work. As the Democratic Convention of 1944 approached, Senator Alben W. Barkley of Kentucky asked Truman to nominate him as vice president, but Truman explained that he had already agreed to support another candidate. Roosevelt, after consulting with the big city political bosses, thought about replacing his intellectual Vice President, ardent New Dealer Henry A. Wallace, with a more practical politician. The President appeared to encourage the candidacy of a number of men, including Wallace, without committing himself to any one of them. He was maneuvering to get a running mate who would bring the most votes to the ticket. The Democratic party leadership was more concerned with selecting a capable man; these politicians knew that Roosevelt was in very poor health and that his vice president would probably become president during the next four years.

In July, Truman arrived at the convention prepared to nominate James Byrnes, the former senator from South Carolina. To his surprise, the Missourian learned that the President might want him to be second-in-command. Nevertheless, he still intended to support Byrnes, for he had given him his word and Truman believed in keeping his promises. However, the Democratic party's national chairman, Robert Hannegan, former boss of the Saint Louis machine, preferred Truman to Byrnes, a lapsed Catholic whose stand on civil rights would cost the party black votes. Hannegan persuaded the President to write a note supporting Truman. The note was released to the press in the hope of weakening support for Vice President Wallace and discouraging the Byrnes candidacy. The note did accomplish those goals, but it failed to persuade Harry Truman to change his mind. Only a phone call in Truman's presence—from Hannegan to Roosevelt—got him to agree to be the President's running mate. The stubborn Missourian commented, "Well, if that's the situation, I'll have to say yes. But why the hell didn't he tell me in the first place?"[12] Truman had enjoyed being an active senator; to him, the vice presidency was a far less important post. He also worried about how his wife and daughter would adjust to the increased publicity.

Fellow Missouri Senator Bennett Clark nominated Truman while Hannegan rallied the state delegations to Roosevelt's declared choice for vice president. On the first ballot, Henry Wallace led, but lacking the support of the big city bosses who controlled many large state delegations, he failed to win a majority of the votes. On the second ballot, Truman won, 1,031 to 105. The crowd cheered and carried on so uproariously that the Truman family needed a police escort to leave the convention hall.

Margaret Truman remembers overhearing her mother ask her father, "Are we going to have to go through this for the rest of our lives?"[13]

In August, when President Roosevelt returned from a military inspection trip to Hawaii, he met with Truman at the White House to discuss campaign plans. They agreed that Roosevelt would stay in Washington to direct the war effort while Truman would travel around the country by train, urging voters to keep Roosevelt in office for an unheard-of fourth term. In his speeches, the Democratic vice presidential nominee contrasted Republican candidate Thomas E. Dewey's lack of experience with Roosevelt's many years as a national leader. The Republican counterattack was vicious, charging that Roosevelt was growing senile and that Truman was corrupt. However, such tactics did not defeat the Democratic ticket; Roosevelt and Truman won by a margin of around 3.6 million votes.

Instead of holding the swearing-in ceremony on the steps of the Capitol as tradition dictated, President Roosevelt decided that the inauguration would take place on the South Portico of the White House. Because the armed forces were still fighting overseas, he did not think that elaborate festivities were appropriate. So on January 20, 1945, outgoing Vice President Henry Wallace administered the oath of office to Harry Truman before his family and 1,800 dignitaries assembled on the White House lawn. After Roosevelt was sworn in, the President, the Vice President, and their guests went indoors to attend a buffet lunch.

Two days after the inauguration, President Roosevelt left for a conference at Yalta with the other Allied leaders; he did not return until the end of February. Within days of his departure, Vice President Truman left the Capitol to attend Tom Pendergast's funeral in Missouri. Despite criticism from the press, he was determined to pay his respects to his old friend. Back in Washington, Truman went through the normal vice presidential routine of answering mail, meeting people, and presiding over Senate debates. His former colleagues found him unaffected by his new position and often dropped by his office for an informal chat. Knowing that the senators thought so highly of his new Vice President, Roosevelt asked Truman to help win their approval for the appointment of Henry Wallace as secretary of commerce.

Harry Truman had been Vice President for only eighty-two days when Roosevelt's death suddenly elevated him to the presidency. He remarked to reporters the following day, "Boys, if you ever pray, pray for me now, I don't know whether you fellows ever had a load of hay fall on you, but when they told me yesterday what had happened, I felt like the moon, the stars, and all the planets had fallen on me."[14]

Over the years, Harry Truman had fought many political battles and had proved that he could make decisions and get things done. In various positions, from county judge to senator, he had shrewdly dealt with some of the most corrupt political organizations of the day, yet had developed a local and then a national reputation for honesty and hard work. Never wealthy himself, this blunt and outspoken loyal Democrat spoke for the common people: farmers, veterans, workers, shopkeepers, and blacks. As the head of the Truman Committee, he had made an important contribution to the nation's war effort by exposing waste and inefficiency. While he could have remained where he was and looked back on his political career with great satisfaction, Harry Truman was chosen to be Vice President and would soon look ahead to the greatest challenge of his life—making decisions as the President of the United States.

THREE

AT HOME IN THE WHITE HOUSE

On May 8, 1945, jubilant crowds all over America took to the streets; shouting, cheering, and hugging one another as if it were New Year's Eve or the Fourth of July. They had just heard President Truman's 9:00 A.M. broadcast announcing that Germany had surrendered. Eleven months after Allied forces had landed on the coast of France, and twenty-six days after Harry Truman had been sworn in, the war in Europe was finally over—although victory in the Pacific had yet to be achieved. The President had two reasons to celebrate: May 8 was not only V-E (Victory in Europe) Day but also his sixty-first birthday. As he wrote in a letter to his mother before the broadcast, "The papers were signed yesterday morning and hostilities will cease on all fronts at midnight tonight. Isn't that some birthday present?"[1] Only the day before, the Truman family had moved into their private quarters at the White House so that they could spend his birthday in their new home.

Sensitive to Mrs. Roosevelt's feelings, President Truman had urged her to take as much time as she needed to make arrangements for packing the family possessions and leaving the Executive Mansion. Bess Truman had also needed time to consult with decorators about the shabby living quarters of the nation's first family. The private rooms the Trumans would occupy hadn't seen a fresh coat of paint since 1933 when the Roosevelts first moved in, and the furnishings were worn out from constant use. To her horror, Bess also learned that the White House was infested with rats.

While the President's official residence was readied for them, the Trumans lived in Blair House, an elegant eighteenth-century home that had been donated to the government to accommodate visiting foreign dignitaries. The Trumans had originally planned to remain in their Connecticut Avenue apartment, but that soon became impractical. The building was besieged by reporters and surrounded by the Secret Service, who demanded identification from the other tenants each time they entered the premises. From Blair House, it was just a short walk across the street to the White House, but Harry Truman soon had to abandon his early morning stroll to work because he attracted too much attention and tied up traffic. He reluctantly agreed to be driven to his West Wing office every day until the family could move into the White House.

Although Harry Truman was humbled by the enormity of the presidential responsibilities he had just inherited and realized that he could not avoid being compared unfavorably with his predecessor, he was determined to do his best. Truman had a portrait of Franklin Roosevelt placed on the wall near his desk in the Oval Office and often stated, "I'm trying to do what he would like."[2] Unfortunately, Roosevelt had never confided to him what his wishes were. While Truman often deferred to his predecessor, admiring his achievements and invoking his name for the sake of continuity, he refused to become a caretaker president, blindly depending on those who had been close to the late president to tell him what Roosevelt would have done. Too often, the late president had not issued clear directives, preferring to play one adviser against another while he awaited developments. Although he lacked inside information about Roosevelt's plans and intentions, before he could act, Truman had to learn as much as he could about his predecessor's policies. Top government officials briefed him on the progress of the war as well as on major foreign and domestic problems, and he read piles of reports as he prepared to tackle the important issues that awaited his decisions.

Now that he had assumed the constitutional responsibilities of his office, Truman was determined to leave his own mark on the presidency, a fact he had made clear at his first cabinet meeting when he asserted his right to make his own decisions. He gradually filled the cabinet with his own appointees, surrounding himself with men he could trust, men who had confidence in his abilities and were personally loyal to him. He recruited James Byrnes as his secretary of state, Lewis Schwellenbach as secretary of labor, Bob Hannegan as postmaster general, Tom Clark as attorney general, Clinton Anderson as secretary of agriculture, and Fred Vinson, first as secretary of the treasury and later, in 1946, as chief justice of the Supreme Court. The president asked his former high school classmate, Charlie Ross, to serve as his press secretary. He gave the post of military aide to Harry Vaughan, a buddy from his army days and the former administrative assistant of his Senate office.

Truman did not have a vice president to help him deal with the routine and ceremonial functions of government while he mastered the intricacies of his new position. When a vice president became the nation's chief executive upon the death of a president, he was not expected to appoint a replacement. The office of vice president remained vacant until the next presidential election. Only with the passage of the Twenty-fifth Amendment to the Constitution in 1967 was this situation remedied.

An early riser ever since his days on the family farm, Harry Truman was up by 5:30 each morning and already at his desk in the Oval Office when his aides came to work. As Truman settled in to his new duties, he gradually evolved his own methods for managing his White House staff. Shortly before nine every morning, he summoned them to a meeting in the Oval Office. At this time he handed out assignments for problems to be analyzed and listened as his aides brought up new items that required his attention. During the day they might drop by his office for further discussion. This procedure allowed Truman to stay directly in charge of his aides, to be aware of and responsible for any actions they took at his request. Unlike later presidents who relied on a chief of staff to distribute assignments and control access to the President, he preferred to deal with his staff personally in a more open, casual manner.

Of course, reporters were curious about the way the new President was handling his job. They sought his opinions on the conduct of the war and on a number of domestic issues. They also wanted more information about the first family, but getting it was not an easy task. The new President remembered how the gossips and scandalmongers had preyed on the all too visible Roosevelt family, and he wanted to protect those he loved from that kind of treatment. As he explained to his mother soon after taking office, "I have kept Bess and Margaret out of the political picture as much as I can and I am still trying to keep them from being talked about."[3] Harry Truman had another reason for wanting to shield his family from the spotlight of publicity: Bess's alcoholic father had committed suicide, and one of her brothers also suffered from alcoholism. The President did not want his wife to suffer the pain of having her personal tragedy aired in public, nor did he want the press questioning her about her frequent trips back to Independence to see her family. In the 1940s, habitual drinking was still considered a social disgrace and a sign of moral weakness rather than an illness.

All of the Trumans, in their own way, soon learned to handle the White House press corps. Bess did not intend to become a publicly active first lady like Eleanor Roosevelt, preferring the comfort of her bridge club and her friends to politicking and crusading for causes. While she adamantly refused to hold press conferences, she was willing to supply answers to written questions submitted to her office. She also invited women reporters to tea and attended their luncheons, but they clearly understood that anything she said was off the record and could not be printed. Margaret took a simpler approach to the problem. Soon after her father became President, photographers started pursuing her around George Washington University, where she was a student. When she let them take all the pictures they wanted, they quickly lost interest. She kept her poise despite the publicity she received as the President's daughter.

As a longtime politician, President Truman understood the value of making himself accessible to the press, even though the relationship was not always smooth. He gave weekly press conferences but refused to be quoted directly unless he gave permission. Shortly after taking office, he even invited photographers to accompany him on his brisk early morning walks. As he boasted in a letter to his mother, they soon found they had trouble keeping up with him: "I took the White House photographers for a stroll yesterday morning and most of 'em wore out. I go every morning at 6:30 to 7:00 for a half hour's real walk, usually doing two miles. I told them that I'd let them take pictures provided they walked the whole round with me. Most of 'em made it, some did not. I invited all of them to come again this morning without their cameras but none of 'em did."[4]

In the rough-and-tumble of politics, Harry Truman expected criticism from reporters and columnists and he got it, but he became very angry when political feuds intruded into his private life and hurt his family. For example, in January 1946, Bess and Margaret became the target of Washington columnist Drew Pearson. This self-appointed spokesman for the average American soldier used his weekly radio broadcast to condemn Mrs. Truman and Margaret for occupying a private railroad car on their return trip from Independence. He implied that their selfish act had kept waiting servicemen from getting back to their homes. Space on trains was scarce at that time, but the President's wife and daughter had paid their own fare for regular accommodations and did not reserve an entire car for themselves.

Later, when Pearson came up to Truman at the end of a press conference to present him with a stack of petitions signed by soldiers eager to come home, the President lost his temper, something he rarely did in public. He jabbed Mr. Pearson with his forefinger and yelled, "God damn you, call me what you want—thief, robber—but next time you tell a falsehood about my wife I will punch you right in the nose, and don't think I wouldn't."[5] The columnist apologized as Mr. Truman stormed off. The incident was closed, but relations between the President and the columnist continued to be strained.

Once the Truman family moved into the Executive Mansion, they were thrust into an unfamiliar, formal household with its own routines and numerous servants constantly offering to assist them. They missed the privacy and warmth of their previous homes, where family members did chores and helped one another. Unaccustomed to being waited on, the President felt uncomfortable dealing with butlers, doorkeepers, maids, and waiters. To cut through the impersonal relationships he and his family were supposed to maintain with the White House servants, the President made a point of shaking hands with each new waiter who served him in the dining room. To the amazement of the staff, he even introduced his brother Vivian to the head butler. Unlike the members of some other first families, President and Mrs. Truman addressed each person who served them by name.

The Trumans respected those who waited on them and appreciated their help, but they refused to be bullied by members of the household staff. When the chief house-keeper repeatedly served Brussels sprouts to the President after she had been informed that he detested them, Bess Truman went into action, announcing her intention to review the daily menus with the housekeeper. The indignant servant retorted, "Mrs. Roosevelt never did things that way."[6] A short time later the housekeeper agreed to retire. After that, dinner in the small White House dining room became more relaxed—so relaxed, in fact, that on one occasion members of the Truman family even pitched watermelon seeds at one another in a mock food fight.

Living in the White House was somewhat like living in a goldfish bowl, which was why the President often referred to the Executive Mansion as the "Great White Jail." Surrounded by a household staff, the Secret Service, and reporters, the Trumans found that they had little privacy. As a result, the President was always looking for ways to make the White House a more agreeable place for his family to live. In late 1947 he came up with the idea of adding a balcony to the South Portico so that he could relax outdoors, away from public scrutiny, with his wife and daughter. The Trumans had always enjoyed the time they spent sitting on the back porch at 219 North Delaware Street, protected from the curious stares of their neighbors. This proposal created enormous controversy, drawing criticism from Representative Frederick A. Muhlenberg of Pennsylvania, himself an architect, from the Fine Arts Commission, and from the editorial writers of the *Washington Post*, who did not want to see any changes made in the landmark building. Ignoring his detractors, Harry Truman went ahead with his plan and had William Adams Delano, onetime chairman of the Fine Arts Commission, prepare the blueprints. Construction was completed, and presidential families since the Trumans have made use of the Truman balcony.

Of course, as President and First Lady, the Trumans

were expected to appear before the public at numerous state functions. The presidential couple found that they had to follow protocol and precedence, the rules governing etiquette and who goes first. Elaborate procedures governed the visits from foreign dignitaries, from the exchange of official greetings to seating arrangements at the table. Preparations for such visits resembled a rehearsal for a formal wedding, although the events being orchestrated often lasted longer and were far more complicated. Three weeks after moving into the White House, the Trumans were given a six-page memo, instructing them on every move they would be expected to make during the visit of an Iraqi prince to the White House. Their instructions included who should be introduced to whom, where they should stand, and when Bess should serve tea.[7] Harry and Bess recognized that all the pomp and display were a sign of respect for the presidential office, and Bess was gradually able to overcome her reluctance to participate in official ceremonies.

The Trumans had lived in the nation's capital since 1935, but they had steered clear of Washington's high society. Although they preferred small parties and casual gatherings of friends to the lavish formal evenings favored by socialite hostesses and foreign diplomats, they graciously accepted the social demands of their new position. Reviving a full schedule of state dinners during the winter of 1946, the Trumans proved that they could entertain with dignity and style. Preceded by a color guard of servicemen carrying flags, the President and First Lady, dressed in evening clothes, led a procession of cabinet officials and their wives down the grand staircase. The Trumans took their places beneath a chandelier in the Blue Room, where they shook hands and exchanged polite phrases with a thousand or so guests who waited in the receiving line to meet the presidential couple. Then the guests filed into the Red Room to be greeted by members of the cabinet. Afterward they all took their seats in the State Dining

Room for a formal dinner, and a Marine Corps band played music until midnight.

Some of the President's official appearances were much more informal, however. Ever since William Howard Taft tossed out a ball on the opening day of the baseball season in 1909, presidents had been expected to continue that tradition. Although Bess Truman was an ardent baseball fan, the President never shared her enthusiasm for the national pastime. Nevertheless, he was determined to meet his responsibilities. The southpaw President showed up at Griffith Stadium to throw out the first pitch at the Washington Senators' opening games, and occasionally he allowed his wife to drag him to the ballpark to watch a few innings of play.

President Truman had other ideas about how he could best relax and enjoy himself away from the pressures of his office and the formality of the White House. He liked to spend weekends playing poker and discussing politics with his friends aboard the presidential yacht *Williamsburg.* Sometimes he simply went to a friend's home for an evening at the card table. In the company of his male friends, he could escape the pressures of his office and feel free to express himself in blunt and salty language. Brought up to be polite and courteous in front of women, Harry Truman could let his guard down only when they weren't around. Among those he regularly invited to join him were his favorite poker-playing companion, Treasury Secretary Fred Vinson, as well as Secretary of Agriculture Clinton Anderson, Missouri Senator Stuart Symington, Secretary of the Democratic National Committee George Allen, and Special Counsel Clark Clifford.

In November 1946, Harry Truman boarded the presidential plane—known as the Sacred Cow, not Air Force One—and took off with friends for the first of many vacations at a submarine base in Key West, Florida. Key West had not yet become a popular tourist mecca but was merely a shabby fishing town full of sleazy bars crammed with sailors on leave. One highlight of the trip occurred when Harry Truman and aide Clark Clifford went aboard a captured German submarine which, much to the dismay of the Secret Service, submerged and took them to a depth of 440 feet.

Even with the ever-present Secret Service and phone links to Washington, the President made sure that the routines at the "Little White House" in Key West were more relaxed than those he followed in the Executive Mansion. He slept a little later in the morning, swam, read the newspapers and the mail over breakfast, and rested on the beach. After lunch he would take a nap, talk with his friends until dinner, and play cards or talk some more until bedtime. Sometimes he went fishing with a friend. On occasion, Bess and Margaret came down from Washington to join him. Of course reporters were always lurking in the background, but they respected the President's need for privacy. At photo opportunities, Harry Truman posed for picture after picture in the colorful tropical print shirts he loved to wear; this delighted the public.

For the Trumans, living in the White House presented far more serious problems than the demands of protocol and the lack of privacy. Living in the Executive Mansion was actually hazardous because the building was on the verge of collapse. A year after the Trumans moved in, the President noticed a hole in the corridor outside his study and ordered the necessary repairs. He repeatedly asked the Commission of Grounds and Buildings to examine the condition of the White House, but they procrastinated. Then, in 1947, Truman observed that a chandelier started to sway during a state reception when the color guard stamped to attention. Only a few weeks later, the floor of his study wobbled when the butler came in with the President's breakfast. The former Jackson County judge finally persuaded the government engineers to look into the problem and described their findings in a letter to his sister Mary Jane: "I've had the second floor where we live examined—and it is about to fall down! The engineer said that the ceiling in the state dining room only stayed up from force of habit!"[8]

For months the family living quarters were crowded with pipes and lumber as attempts were made to shore up the building. Harry Truman even had to abandon his bedroom and bathroom when these were declared unsafe. At the same time, the President appointed a committee of experts to examine the entire structure and make recommendations. They concluded that the White House would have to be gutted and rebuilt and that only the exterior walls could be saved. Before reconstruction could begin, all the furniture and decorations in the Executive Mansion had to be cataloged, packed up, and removed. Little did the President know when he proposed to add a balcony to the South Portico of the White House that he would soon preside over an overhaul of the entire building and that Blair House would be his official residence for three more years.

Harry Truman had made his own mark on the White House, changing it into a more comfortable and private dwelling while accommodating himself to the dignified public life-style his position demanded. Life in the Executive Mansion had certainly presented him with a series of unexpected problems, but he had solved them with the same determination he would show when he faced far more serious challenges. It was his responsibility to bring World War II to a victorious conclusion and to reorganize the government so that the United States would be prepared to take its place as a leader in the postwar world.

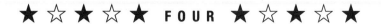

★ ☆ ★ ☆ ★ **FOUR** ★ ☆ ★ ☆ ★

THE ARRIVAL OF
THE ATOMIC AGE

On July 17, 1945, decoding clerks at an American communications center worked feverishly on a top secret message for Secretary of War Henry L. Stimson to be forwarded to President Truman. They were extremely puzzled by what they read: "Doctor has just returned most enthusiastic and confident that the little boy is as husky as his big brother. The light in his eyes discernible from here to Highhold."[1] The mystified clerks wondered if the seventy-seven-year-old Stimson had become a father or if perhaps they had misunderstood the cable and the secretary of war had become a grandfather.

When Stimson decoded the strange message for Harry Truman, the President was overjoyed—and not because his secretary had become a parent or a grandparent. Correctly interpreted, the cable told Truman that the atomic bomb intended for use against Japan would prove just as powerful as the one scientists had recently detonated in a desert site at Alamogordo, New Mexico. The flash from that bomb had been so bright that it could be seen 250 miles away—the distance between Washington, D.C., and Stimson's Highhold estate on Long Island, New York. This cable followed an earlier one, issued on July 16, which had informed President Truman that the United States had successfully exploded its first atomic bomb. Still, the President required more details about the new weapon before he would make the final decision on whether to use it. On July 21 he got what he wanted—a thirteen-page report with dramatic descriptions of the explosion and detailed photographs of the damage the bomb had done to the test site.

Until a few hours after his inauguration, President Truman had not known what was going on at the top secret Manhattan Project, where scientists, engineers, and technicians were pooling their knowledge in an effort to produce the world's first nuclear weapon. As chairman of the Truman Committee in the Senate, he had not questioned Secretary Stimson's decision to bar his investigators from the project's many laboratories and plants, which were scattered about the nation from Hanford, Washington, to Oak Ridge, Tennessee, to Los Alamos, New Mexico. In 1944, House Speaker Sam Rayburn and the House majority and minority leaders John McCormack and Joseph Martin had been informed of the plan because they had to help conceal funding for it, and they were sworn to secrecy. As Vice President, Truman was kept in the dark since Roosevelt felt that only those whose help was needed should be told. For the same reason, the existence of the Manhattan Project was also withheld from General Douglas MacArthur, Admiral Chester Nimitz, and other top military leaders.

Even during the first few days of his own presidency, Harry Truman failed to grasp the significance of the atomic bomb. After Truman's first cabinet meeting on April 12, Secretary of War Henry Stimson stayed behind to talk with the newly installed President about the development of a weapon with enormous explosive power. Since the secretary spoke in general terms, Truman had no way of knowing that Stimson was describing an atomic bomb. Only after Truman had had time to adjust to his new duties did the secretary request a lengthier meeting to discuss the matter.

On the President's twelfth day in office, Stimson

briefed him on the history of the secret effort to build a bomb. The secretary of war mentioned that the United States was cooperating with the British by pooling research, that $2 billion had been spent on research and production, and that a bomb would be ready for testing within four months. He recommended that Truman set up what became known as the Interim Committee, a group of top officials assisted by a panel of scientists, to study how the weapon could be used and to advise the President. Truman approved the proposal. Then General Leslie Groves, coordinator for the Manhattan Project, was introduced to the President and presented him with a twenty-four-page technical summary of the Manhattan Project's accomplishments. Truman, Stimson, and Groves then went over the report together.

On June 1, Truman received the Interim Committee's report. It recommended that the bomb be used against a previously undamaged military target without prior warning. Members of the committee reasoned that only by choosing an intact target would the Japanese understand the power of the new weapon. A prior warning was ruled out lest the Japanese transfer American prisoners of war to the drop site. Also rejected was a proposal to give Japanese officials a demonstration test of the bomb, since the United States would have only two bombs by August, and no one could absolutely guarantee that these would work.

Some scientists working on the Manhattan Project had been debating whether the United States should become the first nation to use a nuclear weapon against an enemy without any warning. Leo Szilard, who had helped persuade Roosevelt to build the bomb, drew up a petition, signed by seventy scientists, expressing their reservations. According to the scientists' reasoning, Americans had begun to work on the bomb out of fear that the Germans were developing their own atomic weapons. However, once Germany surrendered, specially trained investigators sent to capture and detain German nuclear scientists discovered that the Germans had made very little progress in their atomic research. Now the scientists questioned whether nuclear weapons should be unleashed against Japan. Raids by B-29s using incendiary bombs had already set fire to many Japanese cities and had caused widespread property damage and extensive loss of life. Looking toward the future, the scientists went on to predict the coming of a nuclear arms race unless effective international control of this destructive force could be established. However, their views never reached the President because the petition arrived after Truman had left for Europe. Nor did Truman see the results of a poll of 150 scientists at the Chicago Metallurgical Laboratory, associated with the Manhattan Project, where 87 percent of those questioned favored dropping the bomb on Japan.[2]

As American forces drew closer to the Japanese home islands, the battle statistics Truman received grew increasingly grim. The capture of Iwo Jima at the end of March 1945 resulted in the death of 6,281 Americans and 21,000 Japanese; an additional 20,000 Americans were wounded.[3] In June, the battle for Okinawa cost 12,000 American and 110,000 Japanese lives, while 38,000 Americans were wounded.[4] Truman's military advisers did not think a blockade and continuous air raids would persuade the Japanese to surrender. They estimated that millions of lives would be lost in an attempt to land troops in Japan. As the battles at Iwo Jima and Okinawa had demonstrated, the Japanese were determined fighters who would resist invasion, even resorting to suicidal attacks by kamikaze pilots. Determined to save lives, President Truman became more and more inclined to use the atomic bomb against Japan if the testing was successful.

On July 7, Truman left the United States for an Allied conference in Potsdam, Germany, to meet with British prime minister Winston Churchill and Soviet leader Joseph Stalin. He timed his trip to coincide with the atomic bomb test planned for mid-July. In the event that the test failed, he would have to persuade Stalin to enter the war against Japan to end the conflict more quickly. It was a prospect the President did not relish, because the wily Soviet dictator was a difficult man who could not be relied upon to keep his word. By now Truman had learned that instead of holding free elections to let the people choose their own leaders, Soviet troops were setting up puppet governments in the Eastern European nations they had liberated from German control, in defiance of the Yalta agreements. The Potsdam conference had been called to discuss postwar arrangements and to get the Soviet government to honor its promises regarding Eastern Europe. There is no clear evidence that the President hoped to use news of the atomic bomb as a means of pressuring the Soviet leader to cooperate.[5] However, on July 16, when Secretary of War Stimson first sent him the news that the Alamogordo test had been successful, Truman was indeed relieved that he would not need Stalin's help to defeat Japan. Of course, Churchill, long suspicious of Stalin's motives, was also delighted by the success of the secret British-American project.

Earlier, on July 12, United States intelligence had intercepted a message from the Japanese foreign minister to the Japanese ambassador in Moscow, stating that the emperor wanted to end the war and would send a special envoy to Moscow to discuss the terms Japan would accept. They also decoded the ambassador's reply, which maintained that as long as the Japanese rejected the Allied demand for an "unconditional surrender" and insisted on retaining their emperor as sovereign, the negotiations would be fruitless. Given their memories of Japanese peace talks on the eve of Pearl Harbor, American officials regarded the messages as a tactic to divide the Allies when they met at Potsdam. At the conference, although Stalin showed the peace feelers to the supposedly uninformed Truman, little credence was given to them.

On July 22, the President met with his military advisers in his Potsdam lodgings and reviewed possible ways of ending the war with Japan. It can be argued that having the bomb created a momentum for using it. As Truman later wrote, "The final decision of where and when to use the atomic bomb was up to me. Let there be no mistake about it. I regarded the bomb as a military weapon and never had any doubt that it should be used."[6] Truman issued orders to the United States Army's Strategic Air Forces to drop the bomb the week of August 3. Four possible target cities were listed: Hiroshima, Nagasaki, Kokura, and Niigata. The choice would depend on weather conditions. Stimson had urged Truman to spare Kyoto because of its cultural treasures and historic shrines, and the President had complied.

On July 24, Truman casually but deliberately remarked to Stalin that the United States possessed a new destructive weapon. The seemingly indifferent Soviet leader stated that he hoped it would soon be used against Japan. Through his network of spies, Stalin had known about the development of the bomb far longer than had Truman. Two days later Truman released the Potsdam Declaration, urging the Japanese to surrender or face "prompt and utter destruction."[7] In keeping with the Interim Committee's recommendation, no specific mention of nuclear weapons was made. Stalin did not sign the declaration, since the Soviet Union had not yet declared war on Japan, nor did he indicate that he was aware the weapon that would wreak such swift devastation on the Japanese was an atomic bomb.

On August 6, a B-29 bomber, the *Enola Gay*, released an atomic bomb over the city of Hiroshima, producing an unfamiliar mushroom-shaped cloud over the target area. In an instant, a five-square-mile section of the city was reduced to rubble, and wreckage covered an additional ten-mile area. The blast and fire devastated the city, and approximately 80,000 people lost their lives.[8] Yet even then the Japanese did not concede defeat.

Harry Truman learned of the Hiroshima bombing

while returning to the United States on board the warship *Augusta*. Handed the cable while he was eating lunch with the ship's crew, the excited President pushed his food aside, jumped up, and made a brief announcement to the enlisted men. As they cheered, he rushed to the officers' wardroom and repeated the news. "We have just dropped a bomb on Japan which has more power than twenty thousand tons of TNT. It was an overwhelming success. We won the gamble."[9]

On August 8, the Soviet Union finally declared war on Japan; the Japanese still did not give up. The next day another bomb was dropped, this time on Nagasaki, the second site listed in Truman's orders to the U.S. Army Air Force. About 45,000 residents of Nagasaki[10] were killed, but because steep hills confined the blast, the destructive force of the explosion was less widespread than in Hiroshima. As the effects of radiation were felt, the death toll in Hiroshima and Nagasaki rose even higher.

On August 9, a more somber Truman wrote a letter to a member of the clergy, defending his decision to deploy nuclear weapons against Japan: "Nobody is more disturbed over the use of the Atomic bomb than I am but I was greatly disturbed over the unwarranted attack by the Japanese on Pearl Harbor and their murder of prisoners of war. The only language they seem to understand is the one we have been using to bombard them."[11] As the President expected, it took this powerful and tragic display of American power to persuade the Japanese government to end the war. On August 10, after reports filtered in from Nagasaki, the emperor insisted that his nation surrender. Even after this, though, the war dragged on until Japan agreed to the terms Truman stipulated in consultation with the Allies. Finally, on August 14, the United States formally accepted the Japanese surrender with the understanding that the emperor would no longer lead his nation but would serve only as a figurehead.

A *Fortune* magazine poll taken a few months after Japan capitulated showed that three-fourths of those questioned approved of Truman's decision to use atomic weapons, and nearly a third had wanted the Japanese to suffer even more before they surrendered. Only one-fifth had any doubts about dropping nuclear weapons on Japan.[12]

When he authorized the use of atomic bombs against Japan, President Truman had made perhaps the most important decision of his administration, a decision that ushered in a new age and new responsibilities. Nuclear weapons radically changed the nature of warfare; whole cities and thousands of lives could be wiped out in just an instant. Truman realized that while the United States had a monopoly on nuclear bombs, scientists all over the world would sooner or later unlock the secrets of atomic fission and begin to produce the bomb for their own nations. Worried about the spread of nuclear weapons, he wrote, "I now had a responsibility without precedent in history. The decisions I had to make and the policies I would recommend to Congress on the use and control of atomic energy could well influence the course of civilization."[13]

In several speeches during the fall of 1946, Truman advocated international control over atomic energy and instructed the United States delegation to the United Nations to help establish a United Nations Commission on Atomic Energy. This was accomplished in January 1946. Since the commission was scheduled to meet in June, the American government quickly formulated some concrete proposals to give substance to the President's idea. Secretary of State Byrnes appointed a committee to prepare a workable plan. In what became known as the Acheson-Lilienthal Report, the committee recommended that the UN agency take over ownership of the raw materials needed to produce nuclear energy, operate the weapons production plants, direct research, and license nuclear activities. No individual nation would be permitted to manufacture atomic bombs, but until the international body was functioning, the United States would be permitted to keep its stockpile of nuclear weapons.

To present the American plan to the United Nations,

Truman called upon Bernard Baruch, a successful financier and presidential adviser. The President did not admire Mr. Baruch, whom he considered extremely vain, shallow, and long-winded, but he was willing to appoint him as the U.S. representative to the UN Atomic Energy Commission because the press and conservative members of Congress thought Baruch was a wise and dedicated patriot, and they would eagerly give him their support. To soothe Baruch's ego, the Acheson-Lilienthal Report became the Baruch Plan, and Truman permitted Baruch to introduce it to the public. Over the objections of Dean Acheson and David Lilienthal, Baruch added to the original report a section that penalized any nation that violated the international agreement. The Soviet delegate to the UN Commission found this provision particularly offensive and seized on it as an excuse to reject the entire American plan. He offered a counterproposal, that the United States destroy its own nuclear stockpile before international controls were even discussed. Of course the United States found this suggestion unacceptable. The Soviet government had no intention of halting its own crash program to produce nuclear weapons, so the two sides quickly became deadlocked, and the arms race began in earnest. Significant mutual reduction of atomic stockpiles would have to wait for some forty years, until the two nations finally signed the 1988 Intermediate Nuclear Forces Treaty to eliminate some short- and medium-range nuclear missiles. Even greater reductions were made in 1992 after the Soviet Union was dissolved into the Commonwealth of Independent States. At that juncture, the prospect of international control of atomic energy seemed less remote.

Once the war was over, Truman also had to decide whether civilian or military personnel should take charge of the American nuclear program. The President felt that the power of the atom should be used for peaceful as well as destructive purposes, and hoped that private companies might find new ways to harness atomic energy for the public good. Although the American military had sponsored the development of a nuclear bomb, Truman preferred to let civilians control future applications of nuclear power—even though he knew he would have a fight on his hands. Right after the Japanese surrender, military leaders tried to get Congress to create a permanent "Manhattan District," modeled on the Manhattan Project, with an army general in charge of civilian scientists, industrialists, and workers. Truman responded by sending a strongly worded message to Congress that emphasized the peaceful uses of nuclear energy and his determination to institute civilian control. What made Truman's position more difficult was the February 1946 discovery in Ottawa, Canada, of a spy ring which had tried to obtain American atomic secrets to pass on to the Soviet Union. Spokesmen for the armed services and conservative members of Congress insisted that military control was the only way to protect such sensitive data. Actually, while General Groves was in charge of the Manhattan Project, spies had already turned over to the Soviet Union information needed to produce nuclear bombs.

Truman continued to support the idea of civilian control, arguing in speeches, memos, and letters that it was a time-honored American tradition. Although he did not dispute the need for government ownership of all fissionable materials (those from which a bomb could be made), he reasoned that science and industry had always made progress when they were free to conduct research and market new products without government restrictions. He wanted private patents to be issued to encourage individuals to devise new ways to use atomic energy for the benefit of all. He anticipated that nuclear power would eventually be applied to such peaceful purposes as the generation of electricity for homes and factories and the creation of radioactive isotopes to diagnose diseases and treat cancerous tumors. On August 1, 1946, Truman signed a law creating the Atomic Energy Commission (AEC), which placed civilians in charge of the nation's nuclear energy program.

Research continued on atomic weapons while, in September 1949, experts from the AEC determined that the Soviet Union had detonated an atomic bomb. By October, some scientists led by physicists Edward Teller and Ernest Lawrence prodded the government to let them work on a hydrogen bomb that would be ten times more powerful than the weapons dropped on Hiroshima and Nagasaki. J. Robert Oppenheimer, head of the Los Alamos laboratory that had produced the first atomic bomb, and other scientists disagreed. They did not think it was either necessary or possible to produce this new weapon. They felt that it was more important to develop and stockpile more powerful atomic bombs. The AEC and the scientific community were divided over the issue. However, the President felt it his duty to make sure that every step was taken to defend the nation, and in January 1950 he authorized development of the new weapon, which was finally tested in November 1952. The AEC continued to guide the development of military and civilian uses of nuclear energy in the United States until the 1970s, when President Jimmy Carter divided its responsibilities between the Department of Energy and the Nuclear Regulatory Commission.

To develop and drop atomic bombs had required the cooperation of the armed services, but such cooperation was not easily achieved. During the war, Truman had often consulted with the army's secretary of war, whose department included the air force, and the secretary of the navy, whose department represented the Marine Corps, to develop a concerted plan of action. This process was time-consuming and inefficient because of interservice rivalries. As a former World War I captain and as the chairman of the Truman Committee in the Senate, the nation's commander in chief was well aware of the waste and duplication during military operations as well as in setting up bases and obtaining supplies. As a result, he became convinced that the organization of the American armed services badly needed an overhaul. As early as the summer of 1945, he began to work on a plan to unify the armed forces into one Department of Defense under civilian leadership and with a single budget. In December he sent a message to Congresss urging the creation of the new department under a secretary of defense who would coordinate the activities of the army, navy, and air force. Truman recommended that the Marine Corps remain a part of the navy, but that the air force become an independent service. However, he soon came up against opposition from the armed services and the congressional committees that protected their interests.

The army preferred a department that would truly unify the services and purchase common equipment for all, while the navy, intent on preserving its freedom of action, was even reluctant to agree to a loose federation of the services. Eventually, after prolonged negotiations, the military services and their congressional defenders reached a series of compromises making possible the passage of the Unification Act of 1947, which established the Department of Defense and separated the air force from the army. Despite further moves toward centralization, the three services remained fairly independent, and a truly unified military program never developed. In a masterful move, the President appointed Secretary of the Navy James V. Forrestal to serve as the nation's first secretary of defense. Truman reasoned that in this post Forrestal would strengthen the new department, but if he remained as a spokesman for naval interests he would obstruct the system and make it unworkable. The President was a shrewd judge of people, and until his untimely death, Forrestal fulfilled Truman's expectations.

Perhaps because he had been the last one to know about the atomic bomb, Harry Truman was determined to ensure that he and future presidents of the United States got all the facts they needed to make decisions and protect the country. During the war, Truman had had to rely on reports from War Department G-2 investigators, Office of Naval Intelligence operatives, Office of Strategic Services (OSS) foreign agents, State Department diplomats, and Federal Bureau of Investigation agents. Since the collection of intelligence data was divided among so many different sources, it was no wonder that President Roosevelt's naval fleet had been caught unprepared when the Japanese launched their surprise attack on Pearl Harbor.

Impatient with cumbersome legislative procedures that delayed his request for a new intelligence-gathering organization, President Truman took action on his own to ensure that he would receive the information he needed. No longer would intelligence reports be scattered among a number of government agencies where they could be delayed or lost before reaching the Oval Office. He also disbanded the OSS as unsuitable for peacetime operations and issued an executive order creating the Central Intelligence Group (CIG) to replace it in January 1946. Under the supervision of a director of Central Intelligence, the CIG was to coordinate the collection and assessment of intelligence reports. This arrangement enabled the President to receive daily summaries of information obtained from abroad and of messages sent abroad. He sent an amusing memo to Admiral William D. Leahy, his chief of staff, and Rear Admiral Sidney W. Souers, whom he appointed as the first director of Central Intelligence:

To My Brethren and Fellow Doghouse Denizens:

By virtue of the authority vested in me as Top Dog I require and charge that Front Admiral William D. Leahy and Rear Admiral Sidney W. Souers receive and accept the vestments and appurtenances of their respective positions, namely as personal snooper and as director of centralized snooping.

Left: *Harry Truman's parents, Martha Ellen Young and John Anderson Truman, pose for a formal wedding portrait in 1881.*

Harry Truman's birthplace was this white frame house in Lamar, Missouri. The mule shoe was placed over the doorway on the day of his birth.

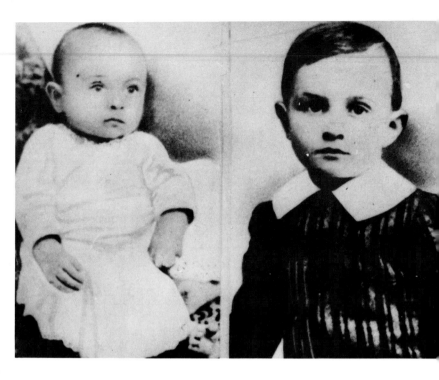

Harry Truman as a baby, at age four, and (below)
with his high school graduating class. Truman is
standing fourth from the left in the back row.
Bess Wallace, who became his wife, is the last
figure at the right in the second row and
Charles Ross, who became Truman's press
secretary, is at the extreme left in the first row.

In 1910, Truman was performing chores on the Grandview farm. In 1918, Captain Truman was serving with the 129th Field Artillery in Brittany.

In June 1919, the former soldier and
Bess Wallace were married.

*Turning from farming, Truman entered
retail business with a haberdashery
that, sadly, failed in 1922.*

*Truman's next position—as county judge in Jackson
County, Missouri—launched him into a political career.*

In 1940, with one senatorial term behind him, Truman posed for a reelection campaign photo on the steps of the Capitol Building.

At the 1944 Democratic National Convention, Harry Truman, seated between Bess and Margaret Truman, was nominated for the vice presidency.

*In August 1944, the vice-presidential
candidate had one of his few meetings with
President Franklin Roosevelt, at a White House
luncheon to discuss campaign plans.*

*Just nine months later, following
Franklin Roosevelt's death, Harry Truman
was sworn in as President of the United States.*

*At the 1945 Potsdam Conference, President Truman
took his place among the "Big Three" world
leaders, with Prime Minister Winston Churchill
of Great Britain and Soviet leader Joseph Stalin.*

Twenty-six days after becoming president, Truman was able to announce the German surrender. Faced with the prospect of great losses in the continuing war with the Japanese, however, Truman made the difficult decision to use the atomic bomb. Left: *the mushroom-shaped cloud of an atomic explosion.* Below: *the scene in Nagasaki after the bomb blast.*

On August 14, 1945, President Truman
read reporters an announcement of the
Japanese surrender—officially
signaling the end of World War II.

On board the U.S.S. Missouri in Tokyo Bay, the
Japanese foreign minister Mamoru Shigemitsu
signed documents of surrender as General
Douglas MacArthur, supreme Allied commander,
broadcast an account of the proceedings.

*In the Westminster College gymnasium,
Fulton, Missouri, Truman introduced
Winston Churchill, who used this opportunity
to deliver his historic "Iron Curtain" speech.*

Campaigning hard against Tom Dewey, the 1948 frontrunner, underdog Harry Truman whistle-stopped across the country; he captured crowds and votes to achieve a victory that surprised many—including the Chicago Daily Tribune.

Truman's years in the presidency were crowded with historic moments, but events on a more personal scale also attracted public interest. He collected headlines when he angrily reacted to critics of Margaret Truman's concerts. The addition of a controversial "Truman Balcony" to his "Great White Jail," and a later major reconstruction of the building were carefully watched and often discussed. (The balcony is visible behind the columns in the photograph of the White House in the midst of the reconstruction project.)

Among important
developments during
the later years of the
Truman presidency were
the Russian blockade
of West Berlin, which
Truman countered with
the Berlin Airlift to deliver
food and other essentials to
the city's residents (top);
and the U.S. involvement
in the Korean War, during
which he repeatedly clashed
with and ultimately dismissed
General Douglas MacArthur,
the popular war hero and
supreme commander
of the UN forces.

As former president, Harry Truman was able to return home and continue his habitual early-morning walks in the quieter surroundings of Independence, Missouri.

*In 1955, Truman displayed the initial
volume of his memoirs, covering the
frantic early months of his presidency.*

*As an elder statesman, Truman received
many honors. President Lyndon Johnson
(seated at the desk) chose the Truman Library as
the site for the signing of the 1965 Medicare Act,
in recognition of Truman's early efforts to create
a program of national health insurance.
(Harry and Bess Truman are at the extreme right.)*

. . . I charge that each of you not only seek to better our foreign relations through more intensive snooping but also keep me informed constantly of the movements and actions of the other. . . .[14]

In 1947, when Congress passed the National Security Act, the CIG became the Central Intelligence Agency (CIA), with the power to coordinate and evaluate information. It was also directed to perform "other functions and duties related to intelligence affecting the national security."[15] Although some of its "other functions," such as covert operations, have at times brought the CIA into disrepute, American presidents still benefit from the activities of the agency Harry Truman founded.

In the nuclear age, the United States could ill afford to be uninformed about threats to the peace or unprepared to meet them, which explains why Truman asked Congress to establish a National Security Council (NSC) to advise the President. He recalled that at Potsdam, the War, Navy, and State departments had set up a committee that handled problems without the usual interservice fights over jurisdiction. At the end of the Potsdam conference he had asked the three departments to continue this informal committee system, which in 1947 formally became the NSC. Its original members included the secretaries of the army, state, navy, defense, and air force as well as the president and the chair of the National Securities Resources Board. Although membership on the council has changed over time, it still studies potential threats to American security all over the globe and offers recommendations to the president.

In the overlapping worlds of national and international politics, many events take place at the same time. These may require a president to make decisions, but the decisions are not made in a vacuum nor can they be made in isolation from one another. While Harry Truman was negotiating with world leaders at Potsdam on postwar settlements, he was also issuing orders to drop the atomic bomb on Japan and thinking about ways to get his military and civilian advisers to work together. While he was taking steps to encourage international civilian control of atomic energy, he was also urging Congress to unify the armed services, to systematize intelligence evaluation, and to coordinate national security policy-making. At the same time he faced numerous other problems involving the reallocation of people, resources, and industries as the nation moved from a wartime to a peacetime economy. Harry Truman would be asked to solve some of these problems before he completed even his first year as President; others would take more time. However, Truman was willing to make difficult and unpopular decisions and would be given plenty of opportunity to do so.

FIVE

POSTWAR POLITICS OF ADJUSTMENT

On Saturday afternoon, May 25, 1946, a solemn President Truman entered the chamber of the House of Representatives prepared to address the assembled legislators on the measures he would take to deal with the nation's most recent labor crisis. He was not sure how they would react to him or to the steps he had taken to end the work stoppages. To his surprise, the assembled senators and members of Congress welcomed him with a solid round of applause.

The President mounted the rostrum and started to talk about the railroad strike which, for the first time in American history, had brought all the nation's trains to a standstill. This 1946 railroad strike paralyzed the country and strangled the nation's commerce by choking off deliveries of mail, food, raw materials, and finished products (long-distance interstate trucking and air freight shipments had not yet become an important part of the American transportation system). The legislators listened intently as Truman, speaking in plain language, reviewed his reasons for seizing the railroads and placing them under temporary government ownership. Infuriated by the railroad labor leaders' obstinate refusal to accept the wage increase the government had offered them, he harshly condemned them for going on strike.

Meanwhile, in another part of the Capitol building,

Truman's special counsel, Clark Clifford, waited impatiently for an important phone call, hoping to get word that the crisis had been resolved. When the phone rang, he picked up the receiver and heard a voice on the other end exclaim, "We have reached an understanding! The strike is broken! The men are going back!"[1] He quickly copied the message onto a piece of paper and turned it over to Leslie Biffle, secretary of the Senate, who dashed over to the House chamber. The President had just announced, "I request the Congress immediately to authorize the President to draft into the Armed Forces of the United States all workers who are on strike against their government,"[2] when Biffle handed him Clifford's note. Truman scanned it and then told his waiting audience, "Word has just been received that the railroad strike has been settled on the terms proposed by the President."[3] A relieved Congress cheered enthusiastically.

In November 1946 John L. Lewis, a controversial and powerful labor leader who was head of the United Mine Workers (UMW), called another dramatic walkout. He decided he was no longer satisfied with the terms of the settlement Harry Truman had imposed on the mine owners in May after an earlier strike when the government had seized the coal mines. The union had been given a pay increase of 18½ cents an hour, $100 in vacation pay, a forty-five-hour work week, and a welfare and retirement fund (a new benefit for those times). However, Lewis stubbornly pulled his men off the job because he wanted his mine workers to have a contract that would take into account the latest changes in government wage policy.

Ever since his days in the Senate, Truman had been contemptuous of the mine leader, condemning him for calling strikes during the war; now he resented Lewis's attempt to intimidate the President of the United States. Refusing to tolerate such insubordination, he decided to "fight to finish John L. Lewis."[4] The angry President sent Attorney General Tom Clark to federal court to charge the

UMW with violating the Smith-Connally Act, a law banning strikes in federally seized industries. Finding for the government, Judge Alan Goldsborough issued an injunction that directed the union leader to call off the strike. When Lewis defied the court order, the judge fined him $10,000 and his union $3.5 million.[5] Meanwhile the nation was running out of coal, the fuel most commonly used in the 1940s to heat homes, power factories, and run trains. As pressure on Lewis mounted, he tried to negotiate with the President terms for ending the strike, but Harry Truman stood firm and refused to take his calls. Finally, on December 7, Lewis conceded defeat, calling a press conference to announce that his union would go back to work and would abide by the terms of the May contract.

During the war, government boards had instituted wage controls that set limits on earnings, although workers were often able to boost their income by putting in extra hours to qualify for overtime pay. Those extra hours and night shifts made it possible for American factories to speed up production of the arms and equipment the Allies needed. Once the war ended, wage controls remained in effect, but the labor force returned to a forty-hour week and a smaller weekly paycheck. To make matters worse, for a short time, as industries converted from military to civilian production, many workers temporarily lost their jobs. In the first ten days of peace, 1.8 million workers found themselves briefly unemployed.[6]

Although the government had taken over the ownership of steel mills, coal mines, meat-packing plants, and oil-producing and refining plants when labor and management negotiations were deadlocked, this was, at best, a stopgap measure to keep the nation's economy from grinding to a halt. Before the end of 1946, about 5,000 strikes had erupted across the nation. Truman had in mind more permanent solutions to the nation's labor problems, including an increase in the minimum wage (the lowest legal hourly pay an unskilled worker could receive), a higher rate of unemployment compensation for workers who had lost their jobs, and a full employment act. President Truman had wanted the Congress to accept full employment as a national goal, to have the government guarantee a job to every able-bodied person—even if the government itself had to become a major employer. Truman had in mind public works jobs similar to the federally sponsored New Deal programs that had employed people to construct bridges, roads, and public buildings during the 1930s.

In passing the Employment Act of 1946, Congress rejected the goal of full employment and instead directed the government to use its existing powers to prevent serious unemployment. Although the new law fell short of Truman's goals, never before had the government made this type of commitment to its people. Still in force today, the Employment Act also created a Council of Economic Advisors to keep the President informed about economic conditions and to help him prepare a yearly economic report to be presented to Congress every January.

Although Congress passed the legislation Truman had recommended, the legislators were also seeking their own solutions to the rash of work stoppages plaguing the nation. In June 1946 they passed a tough anti-strike bill similar to the one the President had requested in his May 25, 1946, speech. However, once the railroad strike was settled, Truman began to have doubts about the proposed law, believing that it would not prevent strikes and would hurt the growing labor movement. He recognized that strikes were a weapon union organizers needed, to force management to recognize their claims to represent workers and to get companies to negotiate workers' conditions of employment and pay scales. Truman wanted to reform the labor movement, not punish it. He kept the bill from becoming law by vetoing it, or refusing to sign it.

The 1946 midterm elections resulted in a Republican-controlled legislature that tended to be more sympathetic to business interests than to labor's needs. Joining forces with southern Democrats who shared their conservative outlook, congressional Republicans decided to show the labor movement that it could no longer strangle the economy to get concessions. In June 1947 Congress passed the Taft-Hartley Act, a stiff law to curb strikes. To handle work stoppages that threatened public health or safety, the new law gave the President the power to appoint boards to determine the facts in a labor dispute and it allowed the government to seek injunctions against the strikers. While an injunction was in effect, labor and management leaders were expected to negotiate their differences; if they failed to do this, the President could ask Congress to take steps to impose a settlement. The Taft-Hartley Act also outlawed a number of labor practices, such as forcing employers to hire only union members and striking over jurisdictional matters, or which union was supposed to perform a particular task.

When the more punitive Taft-Hartley Act came to Truman for his signature, the President chose to veto it. The White House had been flooded with mail from labor leaders denouncing the legislation, and public opinion was very much divided. Truman reasoned that labor would be likely to forgive him for his earlier attempt to draft striking workers into the army if he vetoed this law. The 1948 presidential election was approaching, and Truman knew he would need labor's support to win, but of course, in his public statements, the President did not mention this political factor. Instead, he listed all the technical flaws in the law and went on to claim that it would weaken the trade union movement. Following the procedures outlined in the Constitution, Congress passed the law a second time by a two-thirds vote, overriding the President's veto. In a letter to his mother, a very bitter President wrote: "The situation here is very bad. I am afraid the Taft-Hartley Law will not work. But I'll be charged with the responsibility whether it does or does not work. I've come to the conclusion that Taft is no good and Hartley is worse. . . . Isn't it too bad that public men can't always be public servants?"[7] Ironically, Truman was to use this law many times during his administration, and presidents have invoked it ever since.

The strikes were symptoms of more fundamental problems with the economy that the President had to solve. Because the war had ended so suddenly, the Truman administration had had no time to formulate plans for reconversion, switching from a wartime to a peacetime economy. Recalling his own postwar experiences in his September 6, 1945, message to Congress, the President had cautioned:

> *We must keep in mind the experience of the period immediately after the First World War. . . . prices turned upward, scrambling for inventories started, and prices soon got completely out of hand. We found ourselves in one of the worst inflations in our history, culminating in the crash of 1920 and 1921. We must be sure this time not to repeat that bitter mistake.*[8]

The complicated economic changeover presented many challenges to the government, including measures to be taken about price controls, a problem that defied a simple solution. Truman's staff was to grapple with it for many months, and in the short run they were not very successful.

During the war, many items such as shoes, gasoline, and meat were in short supply, so they were rationed. Because these were things Americans needed, families had to pay the price set by the Office of Price Administration (OPA), and they also had to turn in a certain number of government ration coupons, which could not easily be replaced. Since there was so little for sale, people bought war bonds and put their money in savings accounts for future use. When the war ended, they were eager to go on a spending spree, to buy all the things they had not been able to get for the past five years. However, demand for consumer goods exceeded available supplies, and shoppers grew impatient with the shortages as they competed to buy whatever was available. Since it took time for manufacturers to stop making military equipment and start producing consumer goods, business owners wanted greater profits from the consumer sales they could make. They wanted the government to remove wartime controls on prices so that they could charge more for the scarce goods. Despite Truman's objections, sympathetic congressmen continually weakened the powers of the OPA and cut wartime taxes, leaving consumers with even more money to spend. As Truman had feared, prices skyrocketed, and the economy began to experience an inflation, or a cycle of rising prices.

In response, workers demanded that wage controls be lifted and went out on strike when they failed to get the increases they needed to pay the higher prices. However, the work stoppages halted production while consumer demand rose, thereby perpetuating the cycle of soaring prices. Only gradually did industrial production expand, enabling enough goods to reach consumers to stabilize prices. At that point the American economy settled into a period of increasing prosperity.

The Truman administration also grappled with the problems of demobilization, the process of returning members of the armed forces to civilian life. As soon as the war ended, the President and Congress were bombarded with requests from parents, wives, and children to bring their heroes home. Since American service personnel had seen action on five continents, and military installations were scattered over much of the globe, the available troop ships and airplanes could not possibly transport everyone at once. Moreover, some units had to remain behind in Germany and Japan to serve as occupation forces in the defeated nations. While Truman sympathized with the families, he was reluctant to rush troops home from abroad lest rapid demobilization leave the nation unprepared to meet new threats that might arise in Europe.

Remembering his own experiences and those of other World War I veterans, the President also felt that the troops would need time to adjust to civilian life. Although he was aware that World War II veterans, unlike those who came before them, would have the benefits of a G.I. Bill of Rights, he was still worried. The 1944 G.I. Bill offered veterans government loans for starting businesses, building homes, and getting a college education. However, Truman wanted to make sure there would be jobs waiting for them if they chose to go to work, and he had pressured Congress to pass the Employment Act.

Putting aside his own doubts and concerns, Truman soon had to give in to the mounting pressure to "bring the boys home." In September 1945 he announced that the army would discharge 25,000 troops a day and that he expected more than 2 million soldiers to be home by Christmas.[9] When a slowdown was announced in January 1946, discontented American troops based in the Philippines, India, Guam, Germany, Great Britain, France, Austria, Korea, and Japan, as well as the United States, made headlines with their demonstrations and protests. Despite delays, between the summer of 1945 and the summer of 1946, personnel in the army and air force dropped from over 8 million to under 2 million, while the navy was cut from nearly 4 million to 980,000 service people.[10] To keep American defense strong, Truman offered Congress a plan for Universal Military Training, requiring all men between the ages of eighteen and twenty to get one year of basic military instruction although they would remain civilians. Weary of war, the public and their representatives in Congress rejected the plan. To them, it appeared to create a thinly disguised standing army, in violation of American tradition. Instead, Congress passed a very limited peacetime draft law.

In some of his 1945 speeches and in his 1946 State of the Union message to Congress, President Truman outlined a legislative program to help returning veterans and home-front civilians who had made so many sacrifices during the war. Called the Fair Deal, it was meant to be a continuation of social welfare programs associated with Roosevelt's New Deal. Truman asked for such measures as federally funded housing, a national health insurance plan to cover every American citizen, and aid to education. The conservative Republican Congress refused to turn his proposals into law. There was also no public support for the programs. Rejecting further change, people just wanted to go about their own business, and business was booming.

Nevertheless, Harry Truman was determined to bring about change for one group of civilians and veterans—American blacks. Despite persistent and widespread opposition, he continued to champion civil rights for African-Americans. During the war, many southern black civilians had migrated to the cities to work in war production plants; others served in the armed forces. At war's end, instead of sharing in the American dream, they faced segregation, discrimination, and, in Truman's own words, "repeated anti-minority incidents . . . in which homes were invaded, property was destroyed, and a number of innocent lives were taken. I wanted to get the facts behind these incidents of disregard for individual and group rights which were reported in the news with alarming regularity, and to see that the law was strengthened, if necessary, so as to offer adequate protection and fair treatment to all of our citizens."[11]

Although he worked for civil rights for blacks, Truman did not advocate social equality for them, and his personal relationships with individual African-Americans were not always smooth. Back in October 1945 his wife had accepted an invitation to a tea sponsored by the Daughters of the American Revolution (DAR) at Constitution Hall. Then she learned that black pianist Hazel Scott had been denied permission to perform in the hall because of her race. Scott's husband, Congressman Adam Clayton Powell, Jr., telegraphed the Trumans, urging Mrs. Truman to boycott the tea, recalling a similar incident involving singer Marian Anderson, which had led Mrs. Roosevelt to resign from the DAR in protest. However, Bess Truman wired back that while she deplored the DAR's stand, she had accepted the invitation before the incident arose and would attend, since the two matters were unrelated. President Truman wrote a separate note supporting his wife's position. In response, Congressman Powell labeled Bess the nation's "Last Lady." This so angered the President that he refused to invite Powell to the White House ever again.[12]

The President quickly put aside any personal resentment toward blacks who pressured him to advance their cause, and on December 5, 1946, he issued an executive order, bypassing a reluctant Congress, to establish a Committee on Civil Rights. Its long-awaited report, *To Secure These Rights*, issued in October 1947, offered a series of sweeping recommendations, including more adequate protection of voting rights, home rule for the mostly black District of Columbia, an end to legal racially segregated housing, a ban on racial discrimination in the admission and treatment of students, the elimination of poll taxes, and passage of anti-lynching laws. It took another twenty years before most of these proposals became law, and some never did.

The report also called upon the government to set up a permanent Commission on Civil Rights, a Civil Rights Section of the Department of Justice, and a Fair Employment Practices Commission. In 1941, President Roosevelt had set up a Fair Employment Practices Committee "to encourage full participation in the national defense program by all citizens."[13] This committee had successfully negotiated a number of cases of employer and union discrimination; however, many cases were still waiting to be settled when Congress terminated the committee in June 1946 against President Truman's wishes. Truman repeatedly asked Congress to restore the commission, but a coalition of conservative Republicans and southern Democrats denied his requests. Finally, on July 26, 1948, he issued two executive orders, one requiring fair employment practices in the civil service, and the other integrating the United States armed services. He later went on to ban, by executive order, discrimination by contractors and subcontractors working for the federal government.

These were courageous measures for Harry Truman to take in view of the upcoming presidential election, especially in the 1940s when many white Americans were not as tolerant of other races as they would later strive to become. However, since his early days in politics, Truman had shown his commitment to civil rights, and he never abandoned his fight despite the votes he might lose. As he had said back in Sedalia, Missouri, when he first ran for the Senate in 1940: "I believe in the Constitution and the Declaration of Independence. In giving Negroes the rights which are theirs we are only acting in accord with our own ideals of a true democracy."[14] He also asked his attorney general to look into cases of discrimination against Japanese-Americans and was the first president to support statehood for Alaska and Hawaii, both of which had substantial minority populations.

President Roosevelt had left Harry Truman a legacy of unsolved problems but little guidance or direction. Truman inherited a nation at war and had brought it peace. Although he had had little time to prepare for the many postwar problems of adjustment that confronted him, he was prepared to face criticism for his stand on controversial issues, from price controls to civil rights. He even relished a good fight, as long as it was fought fairly, for the principles and policies he wanted. His years of campaigning had taught him to shrug off opponents' attacks on his personal honesty and accomplishments and to fight back. He had to formulate and defend domestic policies, and at the same time he had to find solutions to international problems. Europe was in a shambles and looked to the United States for leadership and help, while American relations with the Soviet Union grew more strained as the two nations found themselves at odds over the future of Germany, Eastern Europe, and the Mediterranean nations.

THE COLD WAR IN EUROPE AND THE MIDDLE EAST

March 5, 1946, was a historic day at Westminster College in Fulton, Missouri. Students, faculty, administrators, and others with invitations jammed into the small campus gymnasium, their faces glowing with anticipation as they waited for Harry Truman and Winston Churchill to arrive. The President of the United States was escorting Britain's wartime prime minister to their school to give an important speech. Before long, Harry Truman actually stood on the platform, introduced his honored guest, and told his audience that he had not met Mr. Churchill personally until the Potsdam Conference, but that he had come to like him very much. After a few more sentences, the President sat down.

A round of applause greeted Churchill as the portly statesman, dressed in vivid scarlet academic robes, rose and walked over to the microphone. He explained to the audience that since a recent election had turned him out of office, what he was about to say represented his personal opinion and not the official position of the British government. Then he proceeded to address the audience, reminding them that he had seen World War II coming, but that people had ignored his warning. Now he claimed that a new danger was looming and eloquently proclaimed: "From Stettin in the Baltic to Trieste in the Adriatic an iron curtain has descended across the continent. From what I have

79

seen of our Russian friends and allies during the war, I am convinced that there is nothing they admire so much as strength and there is nothing for which they have less respect than military weakness."[1] He concluded by urging the United States and Britain to form a partnership, possibly with other nations, to block further Soviet inroads in Europe.

On that day, Winston Churchill added a new phrase to the American vocabulary—"iron curtain"—and also created an enormous furor. When Truman had initially been given a summary of Churchill's speech, he deliberately chose not to read the text, claiming that Stalin would suspect the Americans and British of plotting against him. However, the President changed his mind and read the speech after it was released to reporters during his March 4 train ride with Churchill from Washington to Missouri. He had commented to the former prime minister that "it was admirable and would do nothing but good though it would make a stir,"[2] but for once the normally outspoken President had understated the amount of controversy Churchill's remarks would unleash.

To the public, some reporters, and a few government officials, the Soviet Union was still the valiant ally that had resisted Axis tyranny at a terrible cost in lives and property. People rallied around Secretary of Commerce Henry Wallace, who refused to believe that the Soviet Union was a potential enemy. Arguing that the Soviets were afraid of being encircled by hostile Western powers, Wallace and his supporters accused Truman of having deliberately provoked Stalin by sponsoring Churchill's speech. Wallace urged the President to dispel Soviet fears by treating Stalin with understanding, openness, respect, and trust.

Officially, Truman did not endorse Churchill's views, but he supported his right to present them, much as he also defended Wallace's right to publicize his position. To ease the tension, Truman invited Stalin to Missouri to discuss the Soviet point of view, but Stalin rejected the offer. While the President wanted to be flexible and maintain a cooperative relationship with the Soviet government, as Wallace advocated, Truman knew that relations between the United States and the Soviet Union were worsening. He had been informed of Stalin's February 9 speech claiming that another war was inevitable since the American and Soviet systems were fundamentally incompatible. That may have been why Truman invited Churchill, long suspicious of Soviet intentions, to give the address in Fulton, Missouri. Churchill's remarks could be seen as a trial balloon to test public opinion as to whether the American people would support a tougher stance toward Stalin. Wallace failed to see that conditions had changed since the war and that the Soviet Union could no longer be regarded as a faithful ally. Thus, when he continued to criticize and undermine administration policies toward the Soviet Union, the President demanded the secretary of commerce's resignation from the cabinet, which was received on September 20, 1946.

The Truman administration could do little when Poland, occupied by Soviet troops, was turned over to a government loyal to the Soviet Union. Despite his promises at Yalta and Potsdam, Stalin had not let the Polish people freely decide their own future. And when the Soviet leader started to renege on other wartime understandings, an angry American President challenged him, their first clash arising over a situation in the Middle East. By an agreement reached at the 1943 Teheran Conference, all Allied troops were to be withdrawn from Iran by March 2, 1946. Long after that deadline had passed, however, Soviet forces remained on Iranian soil to enforce Stalin's demands for oil concessions and to back a separatist movement in Azerbaijan, Iran's northernmost province. Only after the Iranian government protested to the United Nations and Truman sent off a stiff note holding Stalin to the Teheran accord did Soviet troops pull out, in May 1946.

Their next confrontation arose over the situation in

the Mediterranean. At Potsdam, the United States and Great Britain had rejected Stalin's demand to participate in the international commission controlling the Turkish straits, arguing that this body of water was already open to commercial ships of all nations. The Soviet Union had acknowledged Great Britain's historic interest in Turkey and Greece but had a long-standing need for warm-water ports and sought Allied support for this objective. Stalin then decided to deal directly with the Turkish government. In 1946, he insisted that a joint Turkish-Soviet defense force should protect the straits. He also demanded that control of the international waterway be restricted to states directly bordering on the Black Sea, which would have left Turkey at the mercy of the Soviet Union and its puppet governments in Rumania and Bulgaria. The United States and Great Britain responded with stern messages to the Soviet Foreign Office, and the United States sent a naval task force to the Mediterranean. Stalin backed down, but nevertheless, with Soviet troops just across the border, the Turks were forced to maintain a huge army they could ill afford.

Having been blocked in his attempt to control the Turkish straits, Stalin turned his attention to Greece, where a civil war seemed imminent. Various resistance movements were seeking to overthrow a right-wing monarchy. The most powerful of these was the Popular Army of the Liberation (ELAS). ELAS was receiving arms and ammunition from Albania, Yugoslavia, and Bulgaria, whose governments took orders from the Soviet Union. Britain had been supplying the repressive Greek government with funds, troops, and military advice, but in February 1947, the British Foreign Office informed the United States that aid to Greece and Turkey would soon cease because Britain could no longer afford to support its Mediterranean commitments.

The British withdrawal from Greece and Turkey served to dramatize two important facts about the postwar world: in 1945 the United States and the Soviet Union had emerged as the world's two superpowers, and they were becoming competitors. As President and as an amateur historian, Harry Truman was well aware of his nation's responsibilities as a world leader, and he recognized that while the United States had distanced itself from world affairs in the past, it could not afford to do so now. He recalled that America's self-imposed isolation from international affairs after World War I had encouraged the Axis powers to take over Europe piece by piece. In his memoirs, he wrote: "This was a time to align the United States of America clearly on the side, and the head, of the free world. I knew that George Washington's spirit would be invoked against me, and Henry Clay's, and all the other patron saints of the isolationists. But I was convinced that the policy I was about to proclaim was indeed as much required by the conditions of my day as was Washington's."[3]

Truman decided to assume Britain's responsibilities toward Turkey and Greece and immediately requested detailed studies of conditions in the two countries from his military and diplomatic staffs. Next he summoned Senator Arthur Vandenberg, Congressman Joseph Martin, and other leaders of the Republican-controlled Congress to the White House, where he briefed them on the situation in Turkey and Greece. For his plan to succeed, he desperately needed their cooperation. Finally, on March 12, 1947, Harry Truman went before Congress and announced a policy that become known as the Truman Doctrine: "I believe it must be the policy of the United States to support free people who are resisting attempted subjugation by armed minorities or by outside pressures."[4] While the President did not mention the Soviet Union by name, the blunt anti-Soviet thrust of his speech was clear to all who heard it. Whether the President overreacted to the threats posed by the Soviet government and whether he overextended American resources by making a commitment to protect free nations all over the globe are topics still debated today. However, at that time, Congress did not hesitate to grant the President $400 million in military and economic aid for Greece and Turkey. The American people and their representatives had become quite suspicious of Soviet intentions and were willing to tax themselves to wage a cold war if that would keep other nations from falling under Soviet influence or control.

In 1946 a respected newspaperman, Herbert Bayard Swope, had coined the term "cold war"[5] to denote the hostile competition, short of actual military engagement, that was developing between the United States and the Soviet Union. By 1947, when this new phrase had become commonplace, the word "containment" also joined the vocabulary of foreign-relations debates. As defined by State Department planner and Soviet expert George Kennan, "containment" meant applying military and economic pressure to confine the Soviet Union within its borders and to prevent its further expansion. The idea of containment formed the basis of the Truman Doctrine.

Britain's retreat from the Mediterranean was to have other far-reaching consequences for the United States. In April 1947, just two months after pulling out of Greece and Turkey, the British government announced that on May 14 it intended to turn over its responsibility for Palestine to the United Nations. The UN voted to divide Palestine into an Arab state and a Jewish state, but the partition was unacceptable to the Arabs who, like the Jews, considered Palestine their homeland. Fighting soon broke out between the two Semitic peoples.

President Truman and his foreign policy experts brought different perspectives to the Palestine problem. State Department officials, fearful of antagonizing the oil-rich Arab states, urged Truman to let the UN exercise control over Palestine. The President, moved by the plight of displaced European Jews who had survived the Holocaust, felt they should be allowed to settle in Palestine.

He feared that if the problem was turned over to the UN, the Arabs would thwart the creation of an independent Jewish state. Nevertheless, the President expected that partition might have to be postponed until peace was restored to the area.

Truman was subjected to heightened pressure from Jewish leaders who wanted him to support immediate partition. They were so persistent and insistent that he refused to hold any further meetings with them. Only reluctantly did he relent when his former haberdashery partner Eddie Jacobson, active in Jewish affairs, asked to visit him. After discussing the Palestine problem with his old friend, Truman agreed to have a private talk with Chaim Weizmann, the future president of Israel, which took place on March 18. The next day, without consulting the President, the United States representative to the UN announced that the government of the United States had withdrawn its support for immediate partition and would instead accept UN supervision of Palestine. In response, a shocked and angry President wrote: "The State Dept. pulled the rug out from under me today. I didn't expect that would happen. . . . This morning I find that the State Dept. has reversed my Palestine policy. The first I know about it is what I see in the papers! Isn't that hell! I am now in the position of a liar and a doublecrosser."[6] Truman had earlier approved UN supervision of Palestine, but only as a temporary measure, not as a substitute for partition. He had also insisted on seeing the UN representative's speech in advance. Like presidents before and after him, Harry Truman discovered that his subordinates did not always carry out his wishes, whether due to misunderstanding, a communications glitch, or outright defiance.

With the deadline for the British withdrawal two days away, the Arabs and Jews continued their struggle while Jewish-American leaders intensified their pressure on the President to support an independent Jewish state of Israel. On May 12, Harry Truman met for a strategy session in

his office with George C. Marshall, who had replaced
Byrnes in January as secretary of state, Clark Clifford of
the White House staff, and other members of the State
Department. At Truman's request, Clifford presented a
series of political arguments on behalf of recognizing the
state of Israel. This upset the normally unflappable secretary of state, who viewed the matter from a diplomatic
perspective. Marshall angrily told the President, "If you
follow Clifford's advice and if I were to vote in the election,
I would vote against you."[7] Marshall, a revered World War
II general and recipient of the Distinguished Service Medal,
was known for his integrity, conscientiousness, and sense
of duty. He was the man Harry Truman most admired and
respected. It pained the President to have to disagree with
his elderly secretary so he quickly ended the meeting,
reminding those present that the responsibility for making
the decision about Israel was his and his alone. To placate
the irate secretary, a compromise was quietly worked out
that enabled the United States to grant recognition to Israel
without having to exchange ambassadors.

Like many at that time who viewed world events
through cold war lenses, Truman was concerned that the
Soviet Union would take advantage of the British withdrawal and rush to recognize the state of Israel as a means
of extending its influence in the Middle East. Committed
to a policy of anticipating and blocking possible Soviet
expansion, he was determined to act swiftly. On May 14,
1948, once the British formally gave up their responsibilities, and only eleven minutes after Israel declared its independence, President Truman recognized the new nation.
The President did not bother to notify American representatives at the UN of his decision since they had gone against
his wishes once before. A few months later the United
States gave Israel de jure recognition, acknowledging that
the United States would exchange ambassadors with Israel. After 1948, the United States continued to support
the Jewish state while at the same time trying to maintain

friendly relations with its Arab neighbors. More often than not, this dual policy proved difficult to implement because relations between the Arabs and Israelis remained hostile and suspicious, each side charging the State Department with showing favoritism to the other.

Britain's departure from the Mediterranean was just one symptom of the basic problems that troubled postwar Europe. Throughout the continent, bombings had left cities in ruins, with homeless families scavenging in the rubble for the necessities of life. Recovery was slow, for most nations had simply run out of funds. In President Truman's words, "People were starving, and they were cold because there was not enough coal, and tuberculosis was breaking out. There had been food riots in France and Italy, everywhere. And as if that wasn't bad enough, that winter turned out to have been the coldest in history, almost."[8]

In the first two years after World War II, the United States had funneled more than $15 billion in aid to these victims of war,[9] but by 1947 the President and his advisers realized that the Europeans needed an even larger, more systematic program to help them rebuild their economies. European recovery was important to the United States, not just because the American public and their leaders were touched by the plight of suffering people but also because distress and discontent were thought to be fertile breeding grounds for the spread of Soviet influence. Also, economists argued that a reconstructed Europe would provide a major market for American products, a view that was never widely publicized during the debate over proposals to help Europe. In drawing up their plan to accelerate European recovery, the President and his staff decided that the United States should act independently of the UN, since some of the nations to be helped were not members of the international organization. They also agreed to invite all European nations, victor and vanquished, East and West, to participate. In addition, the President and his staff wanted the recipient nations to jointly calculate how much money was needed. In this way the United States could remain aloof from European quarrels over the distribution of funds and could avoid charges of trying to dominate Europe.

Although many members of the State Department had helped him devise an aid plan for Europe, President Truman chose to honor Secretary of State George Marshall by naming the plan after him and having him present it to the public. Marshall had first brought the devastating conditions in postwar Europe to the President's attention, and he had worked hard to develop the program for European recovery. Besides, the secretary of state was so universally respected and admired that his personal prestige would help get the Marshall Plan adopted by a Republican Congress intent on cutting taxes and reducing spending. President Truman was often willing to let others have the spotlight and the credit in order to gain widespread acceptance for his important but potentially controversial policies. Therefore, on June 5, 1947, Secretary Marshall announced to the graduating class at Harvard University, "Our policy is directed not against any country or doctrine, but against hunger, poverty, desperation, and chaos. Its purpose should be the revival of a working economy in the world so as to permit the emergence of political and social conditions in which free institutions can exist."[10]

The Europeans asked for $21.7 billion in loans and credits for a four-year period, sparking a bitter and prolonged debate in Congress. Progressives, the followers of Henry Wallace, nicknamed the program the "Martial Plan," claiming that it was directed against the Soviet Union, while conservative Republicans objected to spending such vast sums of money. However, in February 1948, when Soviet-sponsored communists suddenly overthrew the democratic government of Czechoslovakia, congressional opposition to foreign aid dwindled. In April 1948, the lawmakers voted $5.3 billion for the first year of the Marshall Plan. They went on to spend an additional $12 billion between 1948 and 1952, until the European economies were able to manage on their own.[11] Sixteen nations benefited from the program, with Britain, France, and West Germany receiving more than half of the funds.

The Soviet Union rejected the Marshall Plan and forced Czechoslovakia to reverse its earlier position by withdrawing from the program. Calling the program an anti-communist plot, just like the Truman Doctrine, Stalin officially objected to the provision that required European nations to pool their resources, because he wanted exclusive control over how and where Soviet funds would be used. Also, the plan called for an open accounting of how the funds were spent, and as the leader of a secretive, closed society, Stalin would not permit this. The Soviet government established its own recovery plan for Eastern Europe, the Council for Mutual Economic Assistance (COMECON). This reduced still further any existing trade between Eastern and Western Europe and further divided the continent into rival blocs.

Predictably, relations between the Soviet Union and the United States became even tenser in the summer of 1948 when Germany became the focus of their quarrels. At the war's end, the victorious allies had agreed that Germany should be punished and had jointly held the Nuremberg trials, charging top German leaders with crimes against humanity. The United States, Britain, France, and the Soviet Union divided Germany, and its capital city, Berlin, into four separate zones, each with its own occupation troops. An Allied Control Council was established to set common policy, but the former Allies soon proved to have little in common. The Soviet Union stripped its zone of industrial plants and equipment, which it claimed as reparations for the destruction German troops had wreaked on Soviet manufacturing during the war. Meanwhile, in an effort to make their zones in Germany self-supporting, the Western nations subsidized a massive rebuilding program, causing the gulf between German living standards in the Western and Soviet sectors to widen.

In the spring of 1948, after the Soviet Union had

flooded the Western zones with counterfeit money in an attempt to slow down the recovery efforts in those sectors, a crisis developed over British, French, and American plans to reform the German currency. Representatives of the three nations had met in London to discuss a merger of their zones and the substitution of the deutsche mark, a new currency, for the reichsmark, which the Soviets had debased. Stalin feared they were about to form a separate West German government, a move he strongly opposed. When the Soviet representative to the Allied Control Council, Marshal Vasily D. Sokolovsky, demanded reassurance that the Western nations would not combine and jointly administer their territories, the replies of other occupying powers did not satisfy him, and he stormed out of the meeting. The council never met again.

Then Soviet officials notified General Lucius Clay, the military governor of the U.S. zone, that as of April 1 all American civilian and military personnel traveling to or from Berlin would be checked by Soviet guards, that all military baggage would be inspected, and that the Soviets would have to clear military freight trains. After consulting with President Truman, Clay was instructed to direct U.S. personnel to submit to inspection; however, he was to refuse to allow American trains to be boarded. Instead, the American officials would supply the Soviets with lists of train passengers and cargoes. Truman had concluded that the Soviet Union was taking steps to oust the United States from Berlin and possibly from all of Germany, but he would not allow this to happen. On his own, Clay began a small airlift to bring food into Berlin.

In July, once the proposed currency reform was put into effect in the three Western zones, the Soviet Union introduced a new currency of its own in all sectors of Berlin. When the West retaliated by circulating the deutsche mark in their sectors of the city, Stalin immediately ordered a blockade of all highway, water, and rail traffic to Berlin, which was situated well within the Soviet zone. The Western powers had never secured a written guarantee from the Soviets granting access to the former German capital, so the blockade was most effective. After consulting with the newly formed National Security Council and Central Intelligence Agency, the President proceeded to resist the Soviet demands cautiously but firmly. Armed convoys had been ruled out lest they provoke a war with the Soviet Union, but the United States continued to exercise its rights as an occupying power in Germany. Determined to show the world that the United States could be a dependable ally, Truman refused to abandon the West Berliners.

At Truman's orders, General Clay expanded the airlift so that essential supplies could be flown into Berlin while the President sought a diplomatic solution to the crisis. Supplying a city of more than 2 million people was a formidable challenge that required round-the-clock flights by American and British cargo planes carrying at least 3,500 tons of food and other provisions each day. During the winter, the need for fuel increased the daily load to about 4,500 tons.[12] Harry Truman put the crisis into perspective, writing: "The longer the blockade continued, the more the technical efficiency of the airlift improved, and the more the people of Germany looked toward the West to strengthen them in their determination to remain free. Berlin had become a symbol of America's—and the West's—dedication to the cause of freedom."[13] Spurred by the blockade, in April 1949 the Truman administration helped found the North Atlantic Treaty Organization (NATO), a mutual defense pact linking the defense of Western Europe and the United States. This peacetime alliance, the first the United States had ever joined, required member nations to aid one another in case of an attack by an aggressor state. Despite changes, NATO has functioned for more than forty years. The Soviets responded with the Warsaw Pact of Eastern European nations, which was not dissolved until 1991.

Throughout diplomatic negotiations to end the crisis, Soviet representative Sokolovsky repeatedly insisted that the Soviets wouldn't even discuss the blockade unless the Western powers canceled the currency reform, which they refused to do. The stalemate over Berlin was finally broken in May 1949 after the West instituted a counterblockade; this persuaded the Soviet Union to call off its own blockade. Over the 321 days the crisis lasted, the Western airlift had flown in 2,243,315 tons of food and coal at a cost of $224 million. Truman concluded, "The Berlin blockade was a move to test our capacity and will to resist. This action and the previous attempts to take over Greece and Turkey were part of a Russian plan to probe for soft spots in the Western Allies' positions all around their own perimeter."[14] Once the crisis ended, an assembly of the merged West German zones adopted a constitution for the Federal Republic of Germany, which led to the formation of the German Democratic Republic in the Soviet zone. As Winston Churchill had predicted in Fulton, Missouri, an iron curtain descended across the continent of Europe. This lasted until 1990, when the cold war finally came to an end and the two Germanies were reunited.

Having inherited the presidency with little guidance or preparation, Harry Truman led postwar America in new directions. While respecting the past, he would not be bound by tradition, and he refused to let the United States withdraw from world affairs as it had done after World War I. He recognized that, as a superpower, this nation had a vital global role to play even if that involved confrontations with the Soviet Union. With the Truman Doctrine, the Marshall Plan, and the Berlin Airlift, he pledged his determination to keep the peoples of the world free from tyranny and free from hunger. In the November 1948 elections, the American people would have a chance to rate his performance and possibly give him the opportunity to be President in his own right.

SEVEN

PRESIDENT IN HIS OWN RIGHT

When a locomotive pulled the "Victory Special" into the Saint Louis depot on the way to Washington, D.C., Harry Truman was standing on the platform of the rear car, grinning and waving to the cheering crowd. He gleefully accepted their congratulations, for just the night before he had been elected President of the United States. Someone handed him a copy of the *Chicago Tribune*, with the bold black headline, "Dewey Defeats Truman." Beaming, the President held up the newspaper for the crowd to see, while photographers, popping countless flashbulbs, recorded the moment for history.

On election eve, pollsters, reporters, politicians—almost everyone except Harry Truman—went to bed convinced that the Republican candidate, Governor Thomas E. Dewey of New York, would be the next President of the United States. They were certainly surprised when the results of the election were announced, and they simply could not account for Truman's victory. The red-faced pollsters eventually discovered that since they had stopped surveying the public in mid-October, they had failed to detect the massive shift to Truman that took place during the last two weeks of the campaign. The President had beaten the New York governor by more than 2 million votes, winning twenty-eight states to Dewey's sixteen. (Four southern states had voted for third-party candidate,

Dixiecrat Strom Thurmond.)[1] Support from blacks, workers, about half the nation's farmers, white ethnic groups, and the middle class had made the difference. These voters even gave Truman a Democratic Congress to help him carry out his programs.

Back in March 1948, when the President had announced that he would seek election, only 36 percent of the public had approved of the job he was doing.[2] His prospects for victory were so bleak that some liberal Democrats, including Franklin D. Roosevelt's sons, tried to draft World War II hero General Dwight D. Eisenhower to replace Truman on the Democratic ticket. Despite constant pressure from March through July, Eisenhower declined the offer on the grounds that a challenge to Truman's candidacy would undermine the President's authority at a time when the crisis over Berlin required strong leadership. Despite low ratings at the polls, Truman was determined to win the presidency in his own right, and in June he set out on a cross-country train tour to ask the voters for their support. Although she did not like politicking, Bess joined him for part of the trip, as did Margaret.

Harry Truman gave a total of seventy-six speeches before large crowds and small groups, in big cities and little country towns.[3] He was at his best when he spoke off-the-cuff, talking directly to the people and telling them what was on his mind instead of parroting a formal, prepared speech. Using plain and blunt language, he criticized the Republican 80th Congress for failing to pass his domestic programs. This provoked a response from Republican Senator Robert A. Taft, a prominent conservative politician. Taft not only criticized Truman for attacking the Congress but derided him for campaigning at whistle-stops, towns so small that trains stopped there only when the conductor blew the whistle. However, the senator's comments backfired, because Harry Truman gave these localities a new sense of importance when he visited them, and reporters soon began to use the word "whistle-stop" to describe Truman's campaign trips.[4]

Both political parties held conventions in Philadelphia to nominate their presidential and vice presidential candidates. In June, the Republican convention chose Tom Dewey as their standard-bearer and Earl Warren of California as his running mate. This attractive ticket featured two forward-looking, active young governors from wealthy states, representing both the East Coast and the West Coast. In preparation for the Democratic convention, Harry Truman offered the vice presidential nomination to Supreme Court Justice William Douglas, but Douglas refused. Then seventy-one-year-old Alben W. Barkley of Kentucky, a longtime friend from the Senate, phoned to ask if Truman would consider him for the post. The President agreed, and for the first time, a presidential candidate selected his running mate from an adjacent state, without concern for uniting the party by balancing the ticket geographically or politically. In July the Democratic National Convention duly made Truman and Barkley their official candidates, although many convention delegates from all of the forty-eight states thought that after sixteen years of Democratic presidents, the nominees didn't stand a chance of winning the upcoming election.

Harry Truman ignored these doubters and gave a rousing speech at the Democratic National Convention. Taking the offensive, he attacked the Republican 80th Congress for not passing the laws the country needed. As examples, he mentioned their refusal to support farm programs, a national health program, civil rights, an increase in the minimum wage, and price controls. Then he startled his audience by telling them that he planned to call the Congress back into special session in July to achieve what they failed to do since January. When the lawmakers did meet, they accomplished little, giving Harry Truman even more reason to label them the "Do-Nothing Congress."[5] (It is interesting to note that three future presidents of the United States—John F. Kennedy, Lyndon B. Johnson, and Richard M. Nixon—were members of that Congress.)

Not only did Truman have to defeat the Republicans

in November, he also had to do battle with members of his own party. Soon after the convention adjourned, southern Democrats decided to leave the party in resentment over President Truman's efforts to get the convention to endorse his views on civil rights, including voting rights for blacks and an end to discrimination in the military services and in interstate travel. These conservative southern politicians formed their own party, calling themselves Dixiecrats, and nominated Senator Strom Thurmond of South Carolina as their presidential candidate. They were committed to racial segregation, a way of life they had known and accepted ever since the Civil War. At this time, when the "Solid South" was still the backbone of the Democratic party, the Dixiecrats could seriously damage Truman's bid for the presidency by rallying the states of the old Confederacy to their camp.

Truman's campaign received another setback later in July when Henry Wallace chose to run as the Progressive party candidate. While the President was monitoring the Berlin Airlift, a military operation most Americans applauded, the former Democrat and his supporters accused Truman of constantly antagonizing the Soviet Union with his cold war policies. They also felt that he had neglected Roosevelt's New Deal programs, which had brought so many benefits to the nation's workers. Potentially, the Progressives could draw support away from the Democratic party in big cities and among members of the labor movement.

Long accustomed to being seen as the underdog, Harry Truman was not about to give up and slink away with his tail between his legs. He intended to fight the odds and win. On September 17 he took off on a six-week whistle-stop campaign, traveling around the country by train at a rapid 80 miles an hour, in contrast to the more stately 35-mile-an-hour rate Roosevelt had preferred. In big cities, Truman gave prepared speeches at large stadiums and arenas packed with people, but in the countryside, where the turnout was smaller, he used the same technique he had tried out and perfected in June. At whistlestops, he stood on the platform of the rear car and waited for a local politician to introduce him to the assembled townspeople. Sometimes these voters also got to meet "the Boss" and "the one who bosses the Boss," as Truman fondly called his wife and daughter.[6] The President talked with the people about their needs and asked for their support. When he launched into his now familiar attack on the Do-Nothing Congress, someone would usually call out, "Give 'em hell, Harry!"[7] because his fighting spirit appealed to his audience. Later, as the train pulled out, he would lean over and shake as many outstretched hands as he could.

Between stops, Truman was briefed on the latest developments abroad, since world problems did not grind to a halt just because the United States was holding a presidential election. Despite his vigorous schedule, Truman usually managed to take a twenty-minute nap, which he found very refreshing. Reporters and members of the White House accompanying him on his tour of the nation, however, were quite exhausted from their efforts to keep up with him.

In all, Truman made 356 speeches and traveled about 37,100 miles.[8] His Republican opponent gave only 170 speeches and covered a mere 16,000 miles.[9] The contrast between the candidates was even greater than these figures suggest because of their differences in style and temperament. Unlike scrappy and feisty Harry Truman, lofty and aloof Tom Dewey acted as if he had already won the election. Truman's campaign was virtually a one-man partisan crusade, attacking the Republican record and extolling small-town values. Dewey, on the other hand, with the strong backing of the Republican party organization, conducted a leisurely campaign, speaking in vague and general terms. Because all the polls predicted that he would win, Dewey, unlike Truman, did not feel the need to talk about the issues or to defend his party's record. In their appeals to the voters, neither candidate besmirched his opponent's character or abilities; in fact, the two competing nominees rarely mentioned each other.

Everyone expected Dewey to become the new president—everyone, that is, except Harry Truman. So while the rest of the Truman family stayed up late on election night, anxiously listening to the election returns at home in Independence, Harry Truman stole away to a nearby resort to get some sleep. When he awakened the next morning, he was not surprised to learn that he was the victor. As in his 1940 Senate race, he had overcome the odds and beaten a Republican opponent once again.

This time, however, he did have one regret: his mother had not lived long enough to see him sworn in as an elected President. On July 26, shortly after the Democratic convention ended, Truman had been summoned to his ninety-four-year-old mother's bedside. Before his plane landed, he received the news that she had died of pneumonia. He sadly wrote in his memoirs: "When I succeeded Franklin Roosevelt, my mother had so wisely said that it was no occasion to rejoice. . . . But now that I had been elected directly by the people as President in my own right, it would have been a great thrill for her to be present as her son took the oath."[10]

On January 20, 1949, a cold, sunlit morning, Harry Truman took the oath of office as President in his own right. The outgoing Republican Congress had appropriated $80,000 for the inauguration festivities, in expectation that their own candidate would win, and Truman was determined to spend it all.[11] For the first time since the war, the public was treated to a full-scale parade, crammed with so many floats, bands, and veterans' units that it took three hours to march past the reviewing stand. Truman's speech at the conclusion of the swearing-in ceremonies proved even more memorable than the huge celebration that followed, and not just because his was the first inaugural address to be televised.

Family members, friends, officials, and reporters heard him describe four essential goals of American foreign policy. He listed continued support for the United Nations, ongoing aid for European recovery, and further military assistance against tyranny. His fourth point truly won the hearts and minds of his audience. He proposed a "bold new program for making the benefits of our scientific advances and industrial progress available for the improvement and growth of underdeveloped areas."[12] He wanted the United States, through the United Nations, to share its technical knowledge with the free peoples of the world in the hope of raising their standard of living and making them better able to resist Soviet communism.

Since so many people had heard his speech on television, Truman's idea quickly caught on with the public. Along with the newspapers, people began to refer to his technical assistance proposal as "Point Four." The program did not come into existence until June 1950, however, because it took Congress more than a year to transform the popular phrase into a specific law. While Truman had stressed the need to share knowledge rather than money, the program did require funding. Initially, the legislature granted $34.5 million to Point Four, but in 1952 the sum had increased to $147.9 million.[13] At the end of 1952, there were 2,445 American technicians in thirty-five countries working to reduce famine, disease, and ignorance, and thirty-four Latin American, Asian, and African countries had sent 2,862 students abroad to study the latest agricultural, health, and engineering methods.[14] A decade later, inspired by the work Point Four had accomplished, President John F. Kennedy established the Peace Corps to introduce developing nations to modern skills and methods.

During Truman's second term in office, foreign affairs and domestic politics overlapped with dramatic results. At issue was the protection of government secrets from foreign agents and disloyal Americans. In 1949, the cold war seemed to be on everyone's mind once the President revealed that the Soviet Union had detonated an atomic bomb, thus depriving the United States of its monopoly of the terrifying weapon. With the 1950 arrest of Manhattan Project physicist Klaus Fuchs as a Soviet spy, a shocked public learned that Soviet agents had penetrated top secret American installations and were carrying out undercover espionage operations in the United States. Then, after his first trial had ended in a hung jury, came the sensational second trial of former State Department employee Alger Hiss. Earlier, witnesses before the House Committee on Un-American Activities had accused Hiss of having served as a messenger for a Soviet spy ring during the 1930s. Since the statute of limitations had expired, he was brought to trial for perjury rather than spying, and was charged with lying about his role in sending the Soviet Union memos on Japan and Germany. During the second trial, Hiss fought once more to clear his name, but he was found guilty and given a five-year prison sentence. Only in 1992 did the Russian government reveal that a search of its archives had failed to turn up any evidence that Hiss had indeed been a spy.

Although acccusations against Hiss concerned activities that had taken place twenty years earlier, the public grew fearful that spies were still serving in the United States government. Newspapers reported Secretary of State Dean Acheson's statement expressing his intention to stand by his longtime friend Alger Hiss. These reports further inflamed the public and set off unfounded accusations that Acheson might be shielding other disloyal employees in the department. Yet, in 1949, when he appeared at confirmation hearings in the Senate as Truman's nominee to replace the ailing George Marshall, Acheson had testified openly and without incident about his ties to Hiss. Now, just a year later, the climate of opinion had changed. Acheson offered to resign, lest his friendship with Hiss embarrass the President. However, Truman knew what it meant to be loyal to a friend who was in disrepute, having stood by Tom Pendergast when he was sent to prison.

The President insisted that Acheson remain at his post. He admired and respected his highly intelligent, witty, and devoted secretary of state.

After Hiss was convicted, one member of the House Committee on Un-American Activities, Richard M. Nixon, accused the administration of concealing information about the former State Department employee. Troubled by the tactics the committee used, Harry Truman had refused to hand over information they requested of him, and had already begun to prepare himself for future confrontations with the security-minded legislators. He remembered how, during his Senate years, the committee members had made "wild charges" and had "browbeaten" and "falsely accused" witnesses before them.[15] The President readily recalled other times when concern with developments abroad had led people at home to become preoccupied with questions of loyalty and national security. For example, after World War I, when the newly formed Soviet Union preached world revolution, Attorney General A. Mitchell Palmer overreacted and urged the American people to ferret out Soviet spies in the United States. Truman suspected that the nation was about to enter another period of mass hysteria during which the frightened public would embark on a similar "witch-hunt," so he circulated a study of the problem among members of his cabinet to help them to deal with it.

Events soon justified the President's concern. Senator Joseph McCarthy of Wisconsin began to make speeches charging that the State Department was infested with spies. To make his accusation more believable, the senator maintained that he could produce a list of 205 State Department employees who had ties to the Soviet Union. Although a Senate investigating committee found McCarthy's claims to be false, his popularity soared. By continuing to make accusations against government officials, he attracted a large following among right-wing conservative Americans and made newspaper headlines across the nation. He inflamed public opinion for his own advantage by distorting events or damaging others' reputations, thereby becoming a full-blown demagogue.

Some Americans were prepared to challenge Senator McCarthy's assertions, most notably President Truman. At a press conference, he boldly told reporters, "I think the greatest asset that the Kremlin has is Senator McCarthy."[16] The President was widely criticized for that remark, but Truman was never afraid to speak his mind, no matter how unpopular his views. With great courage, he continued to condemn the senator, focusing on his use of hearsay evidence to smear government employees without giving them a chance to clear their names.[17] However, the senator went on grabbing headlines long after Harry Truman left office. Only when McCarthy overreached himself and launched an unwarranted attack against the United States Army did his crusade against suspected communists in government falter. Then he was finally censured by the Senate, an action that hastened his downfall.

Long before the Hiss case and McCarthyism made national security a controversial issue, Truman had taken steps to protect the government from disloyal employees. In 1946 he had ordered a temporary commission to evaluate whether President Roosevelt's loyalty program needed overhauling; he then used the commission's report to modify faulty procedures. In 1947 he issued an executive order requiring every civilian who applied for a government job, whether as a forest ranger or as a member of the Central Intelligence Agency, to agree to be investigated. People already employed by the government had to be listed with the FBI for a security check, and every time they changed jobs they were subject to a new inquiry. This meant that investigators could examine FBI files, military records, and local law enforcement agencies' reports for evidence of suspicious behavior.

If such evidence turned up, the FBI would conduct a more probing examination of the suspect's past. Membership in an organization with communist ties did not automatically disqualify a person from employment, but it certainly did not further an otherwise promising career. Applicants and employees whose records raised doubts about their loyalty had the right to appear before a review board to defend themselves, and the decisions of these boards could be appealed. Since administrators rather than judges conducted the proceedings, not all the rules of law were in effect. For example, employees could bring lawyers with them, but the lawyers could not challenge witnesses who testified against their clients.

Since Truman had already taken steps to remove spies and disloyal Americans from government, he was outraged when Congress passed the Internal Security Act, and he refused to sign it into law. However, in September 1950, Congress mustered the necessary votes to override his veto. The Internal Security Act sought to prevent Americans from belonging to groups with ties to communism, even though the Bill of Rights guarantees citizens the right to form or join groups and to share their opinions with others. At the request of the attorney general, a Subversive Activities Control Board could look into the activities of private groups suspected of having links to the Soviet Union and could determine whether these suspicious organizations were directly under Soviet control, concealed communists within their membership, or induced innocent Americans to serve communist purposes. Penalties were invoked against organizations that fit any of these categories.

The President criticized the measure, insisting that "In a free country, we punish men for the crimes they commit but never for the opinions they have."[18] He doubted that the Internal Security Act would make groups less vulnerable to Soviet penetration, nor did he think that the Subversive Activities Control Board would turn up many spies or communist supporters. "The Communists now began to scurry underground," Truman wrote.

"Through many devices, such as changes of name, of physical appearance, of occupations, and residence, they made it more difficult for our agents to keep track of them."[19] Debate over the efficacy of government loyalty programs continued during the Truman years and carried over into the next administration.

In controversies such as the national security program, which concerned questions of policy, President Truman could accept the give-and-take of politics while he advanced or defended his own views. However, when his family or friends were challenged, he engaged in much more vehement confrontations with his opponents. For example, Truman took great pride in his daughter Margaret's budding career as an opera singer and enjoyed attending her concerts. On one occasion at Constitution Hall she was called back for four encores, but some in the audience felt that her performance was flawed. In his review of the concert, *Washington Post* music critic Paul Hume described her singing in very unflattering terms. Her enraged father wrote the critic an angry letter, containing such scathing comments as "It seems to me you are a frustrated old man who wishes he could have been successful. . . . Some day I hope to meet you. When that happens you'll need a new nose, a lot of beefsteak for black eyes. . . ."[20] Mr. Hume set off a public furor when he had the unpresidential comments printed verbatim in the newspaper. Harry Truman's advisers thought that he had made a serious mistake in sending the letter, claiming that it would hurt his image as President. However, a survey of White House mail showed that 80 percent of the people who wrote to the President felt he was right to defend his daughter.[21]

Truman was also furious when his close personal friend and military aide, Harry Vaughan, was brought before the Senate on charges of being a "five percenter," a lobbyist who charged clients a 5 percent fee to influence the government on their behalf. While Truman's military aide had unwisely done favors for friends and had flaunted his influence in Washington, he never accepted fees for his services. Instead, he collected contributions for the Democratic party from those he helped. It was also revealed that Vaughan had arranged to have a perfume manufacturer send freezers to the President and four other members of the administration. No law then forbade government officials to accept gifts from friends or the public, and Harry Truman himself had received presents such as food, paintings, cigars, and liquor. One recipient returned the appliance, and the freezer sent to the Trumans did not even work. Despite all the headlines charging him with running a corrupt administration, President Truman refused to accept Vaughan's resignation. Loyalty to an old friend was more important to him than his administration's reputation in the press.

There were other, more serious political attacks on the President—assassination attempts that almost cost him his life. At one time, the Secret Service was warned that a lone gunman would try to shoot the President during an Army-Navy football game, so they took precautions. Another time, a group of Palestinian terrorists sent mail bombs to the White House, but these were detected and destroyed before they could do any damage. Then two members of the Puerto Rican Independence party, Oscar Collazo and Griselio Torresola, almost succeeded in assassinating the President.

The President had supported Puerto Rican demands for greater self-government and had named the first native Puerto Rican as governor. He had also extended Social Security coverage to the island's people and had helped them gain more control over local affairs. At the time, most Puerto Ricans were satisfied with this arrangement, although some aspired to statehood. Unwilling to accept halfway measures, the Independence party demanded the total withdrawal of the United States and sovereignty for the island, but it did not necessarily advocate violence to achieve its goals. However, Collazo and Torresola were fanatics. They intended to blast their way into Blair House, the temporary presidential residence, and shoot Harry Truman.

On November 1, 1950, around two o'clock in the afternoon, the President and his wife were in an upstairs room changing clothes before leaving for an official ceremony at Arlington National Cemetery. Suddenly they heard the sound of gunfire coming from the street below. When the President impulsively rushed to the window to see what was going on, a quick-thinking Secret Service agent ordered him to take cover. Unfortunately, the gunmen had managed to kill one of the President's guards and had seriously wounded another before the remaining guards and Secret Service agents shot them dead. Twenty-seven bullets had been fired in just three minutes. Harry Truman commented, "A president has to expect these things."[22]

As President, Truman had learned to expect a lot of things: defeats and victories in Congress, praise and criticism from the press, and gains and losses in public support. He even expected to succeed when everyone else was certain that he would fail. That's why he was not afraid to campaign for the presidency despite gloomy predictions from politicians and pollsters. After he won, he continued to speak out on behalf of the people and projects he valued and had the courage to condemn actions and individuals he could not respect. During his second term of office, there would be many more opportunities for him to speak his mind and make controversial decisions, especially as he shaped postwar policy toward the countries of Asia.

EIGHT

LIMITED WAR
IN ASIA

On Sunday morning, June 25, 1950, the Trumans went about their normal family routines according to the schedule of activities they usually followed when they were home in Independence. Bess and Margaret attended church services while Harry Truman drove out to visit his brother's farm in Grandview, Missouri, and tinkered with the new electric milking equipment. Vivian Truman was disappointed when the President told him he could not stay for lunch and did not offer any explanation. The anxious President did not want to talk about the potentially dangerous situation in Asia that forced him to return to Independence as soon as possible. Despite appearances, this was certainly not a normal Sunday morning for the Truman family. The night before, the Trumans' quiet family discussion had been interrupted by a phone call from Secretary of State Dean Acheson, who announced, "Mr. President, I have very serious news for you. The North Koreans have invaded South Korea."[1]

The division of Korea into two nations was an accident of history. At the end of World War II, as an administrative convenience, the Japanese in Korea had surrendered to Soviet occupation troops north of the 38th parallel and to American troops south of the line. By 1949 all troops had been withdrawn, but the 38th parallel continued to divide the Korean peninsula, as the cold war had rigidified positions. The Soviet Union had rejected a United Nations resolution, presented by the United States, which called for reunification by means of free elections under the supervision of a UN electoral commission. They offered a counterproposal that the North and South Koreans work out their own destiny. This was, in effect, a call to civil war. Since the Soviets denied the UN commission entry into North Korea, UN-sponsored elections were held only in the South, creating the Republic of Korea, which the UN recognized as the only duly constituted government of the Asian nation. The Soviets promptly established the People's Republic of North Korea, which claimed sovereignty over all Koreans.

After Acheson's phone call, the Trumans had remained in Independence, keeping up the pretense that nothing was wrong, so as to prevent news of the border violation from leaking to reporters prematurely. Both the President and his secretary of state felt that reports of this latest North Korean invasion could prove to be a false alarm, since the communist leaders had previously sent as many as 1,500 men on raids into South Korea. Taking Acheson's advice, the uneasy President decided to wait for further developments before returning to Washington. On his own initiative, the secretary of state had already alerted the UN Security Council in case the situation worsened. According to the UN Charter, only the council had the power to recommend sanctions against aggressors, if indeed a war had begun. Acheson soon received a handwritten note of appreciation from the President for his handling of the mounting crisis.

At 11:30 Sunday morning, Truman got the news he dreaded when the secretary of state phoned to tell him that a full-scale invasion of South Korea was under way and that the Security Council was holding an emergency session. By now the story had made the headlines, but the President successfully dodged reporters and was airborne by two o'clock. Because he had had to leave so quickly and inconspicuously, Bess and Margaret as well as some members of the White House staff were left behind in Independence. During the flight, President Truman decided that the United States would help South Korea resist the attack; otherwise no small nation would be safe from threats by its bigger, more powerful neighbors. Truman told himself that World War II had started because the democracies had appeased the Axis nations, letting them overrun many countries in Europe and Asia before finally resisting their demands. He feared that World War III might begin the same way if the United States did not take a firm stand against aggression.[2] Moreover, the Truman Doctrine had committed the United States to contain the Soviet Union from further expansion, whether in Europe or in Asia.

While the President was flying back to Washington, the UN Security Council voted 9–0 to brand North Korea an aggressor nation and called for a cease-fire. The international body had been able to act quickly and decisively because Soviet delegate Jacob Malik had been absent from the meetings in protest over another matter. Had the Soviet Union directed the North Korean attack, Malik would have been instructed to return at once to his post to prevent the Security Council from taking action. As a permanent member of the council, the Soviet Union had the right to veto actions harmful to its interests. Of course, Truman had no way of knowing that the Soviet Union had not ordered the invasion.

Three hours later the President arrived in Washington, downed a hasty dinner at Blair House, and met with his advisers to plan strategy. At the conclusion of the meeting, he ordered all Americans to leave Korea and issued instructions to Douglas MacArthur, the widely acclaimed World War II general now commanding the American occupation forces in Japan, to immediately airlift military supplies to the Korean Army. The President also directed the U.S. Seventh Fleet to patrol the waters separating Formosa and mainland China in the hope that the navy would help keep the conflict confined to Korea. What President Truman feared was that the Chinese would use the Korean crisis as a pretext for starting another civil war among themselves.

Less than a year before, in 1949, Chinese communists under the leadership of Mao Zedong had defeated the Nationalist forces of Chiang Kai-shek, who retreated to the island of Formosa. Although the fighting had ended, the communists looked forward to driving Chiang from Formosa, while the Nationalists still hoped to return to the mainland and regain control. At that time the United States regarded the Nationalists as the lawful government of China and insisted that they retain China's seat on the UN Security Council. It was to protest this policy that Soviet Representative Jacob Malik had walked out of Security Council meetings. Although controversial, United States policy toward the Nationalists was a logical extension of President Roosevelt's wartime plans.

Since Roosevelt had believed that postwar China would become the leading power in Asia, the President and his successor had supplied the Nationalists with 2 billion dollars' worth of arms, funds, and military support to fight the Japanese during World War II.[3] Frustrated American military officers and diplomats sent to work with the Nationalist government soon discovered, however, that Chiang Kai-shek was saving most of the American funds and equipment in preparation for future battles with the Chinese communists. The presence of Japanese troops on the mainland had interrupted a growing struggle for power between the Nationalists and the communists. At the end of World War II, the Chinese Nationalists and the communists had waged a bitter civil war despite repeated American efforts to get them to form a coalition government.

The Nationalists had many powerful supporters in the United States, known collectively as the China Lobby.

Among them were Republican Senator William Knowland of California and Henry Luce, publisher of *Time* magazine, who constantly urged Harry Truman to help Chiang fight the communists. The President was not prepared to order American troops to China, but he did continue to send money and military advisers to the Nationalist forces. He also managed to conceal from the public just how ineffective and corrupt Chiang's government was, even though the disclosure would have helped him withstand mounting pressure from the China Lobby. The President reasoned that exposing Chiang would completely destroy the slim chance the Nationalists had to win the war. The nation's leaders and the press had treated Chiang as a hero and said little about the futility of his cause, which is why the public was so surprised and alarmed to learn in 1949 that China had "suddenly" fallen to the communists. Few remembered that the struggle had been going on for years.

Most American leaders believed that the Soviet Union had plotted the communist takeover of China. Although the Soviets had been supplying Mao's forces with arms and equipment and had let them occupy areas the Soviet army had liberated from the Japanese, Mao would not allow Stalin to control or manipulate him. The Chinese leader and his followers were proud of having formed their own communist movement and went on to oust Chiang's government on their own. What many Americans, including the President, failed to understand was that the communist triumph in China was not necessarily a victory for the Soviet Union. This error in judgment had carried over into initial American evaluations of the situation in Korea and had prevented policy-makers from realizing that the Soviet Union had not masterminded the North Korean invasion of South Korea.

By June 27, 1950, reports from Korea indicated that the conditions had further deteriorated, with North Korean forces overpowering and outnumbering the poorly trained South Korean troops. After another emergency meeting with his advisers, Truman ordered the navy and the air force to support the South Koreans, but he cautioned them not to cross the 38th parallel. In his official statement to the public, Truman also announced that the United States government intended to be guided by UN directives. The White House was soon flooded with telegrams and letters expressing approval for the measures the President had taken. Later that evening the Security Council followed Truman's lead by issuing a call for UN members to help South Korea repel the North Korean aggressors. Soviet Representative Malik hastened back to the Security Council to veto further plans to help South Korea; however, American diplomats learned that although the Soviet government would not help bring about a cease-fire, it did not plan to send troops to support North Korea.

Once he was informed of Soviet intentions, President Truman overcame his reluctance to commit ground forces to the Asian peninsula. On June 29 General MacArthur cabled Washington that Seoul, the capital of South Korea, had fallen and that casualties were very high. Truman immediately instructed American troops to take over and protect the port of Pusan, not yet part of the battle zone, and gave permission for the air force to strike military targets in North Korea. By these orders, he increased American involvement in the war but kept a tight rein on what U.S. forces could do and where they could do it.

At a press conference earlier in the day, President Truman had denied that the United States was about to fight a major war, and although he consulted with congressional leaders, he never asked Congress to declare war on North Korea. When a reporter described the situation as a "police action" enforcing a UN resolution, Truman agreed that UN forces would be "policing" the Korean peninsula to restore law and order. Another new term had entered the American vocabulary.[4] In his public comments and orders to MacArthur, President Truman was doing his best to ensure that American participation in the Korean war was limited both geographically and militarily, which is why he had restricted the zone of aerial warfare first to South Korea and then to military targets in North Korea. In addition, he had taken measures to keep the Nationalist and communist Chinese isolated from the situation and from each other. To confine the conflict, the President would have to make other, more difficult decisions, and he would not always be successful. After all, his administration was the first to attempt to fight a limited war in the atomic age, and trial and error was his only guideline.

Early on the morning of June 30, after returning from a personal inspection of the battlefront, MacArthur cabled that unless the United States government was prepared to move in American ground forces immediately, South Korea would fall to the communists. Harry Truman told the general to use all troops under his command, including combat soldiers stationed in Japan, but at the same time the President avoided the risk of widening the war by rejecting an offer from Chiang Kai-shek to send 33,000 Chinese troops to Korea. Eventually, forty-two other nations contributed money, supplies, or personnel to the conflict,[5] but the American armed services made up four-fifths of the UN forces in Korea.[6] Under these circumstances, President Truman assumed primary responsibility for the conduct of the war.

After a difficult summer of bitter fighting, General MacArthur rallied his forces and stopped the North Korean advance at the city of Pusan, on the southernmost edge of the peninsula. Then, on September 15, with the reluctant blessing of the President and his military advisers, the general launched a clever but risky plan to land troops deep in enemy-held territory at Inchon, a major seaport 200 miles northwest of Pusan. Because the maneuver succeeded, MacArthur was able to cut off North Korean lines of communication and trap the communist troops between Inchon and Pusan, forcing them to flee northward, toward the 38th parallel. The President sent MacArthur a congratulatory telegram.

With the North Koreans in retreat, U.S.-UN forces

were tempted to pursue the enemy across the 38th parallel. Although Truman did not want to provoke the Soviets or the communist Chinese into entering the conflict, he came under pressure from Congress and the public to take advantage of the new situation and try to reunify Korea. After meeting with his National Security Council, the President issued orders permitting MacArthur to conduct military operations north of the 38th parallel, but he was emphatic in insisting that no troops were to cross into provinces bordering on the Soviet Union or China. The UN General Assembly passed a vaguely worded resolution on October 7 in support of the President's decision.

Throughout the month of October, U.S.-UN troops drove the enemy forces farther and farther up the peninsula, capturing the North Korean capital of Pyongyang with little opposition. Chinese communist soldiers were just beginning to turn up among the prisoners of war taken by the victors, but these were thought to be volunteers. As a result, MacArthur continued to underestimate the risk of full-scale Chinese intervention and to relay this view to Washington. On November 6 he asked for permission to bomb the bridges that spanned the Yalu River, separating North Korea from China, to halt the flow of enemy troops and supplies. Truman consented, but he placed the Chinese side of the bridges off limits to the bombers. The next day, the President refused MacArthur's request to pursue enemy planes into Chinese territory, since he feared that the Soviets or the Chinese might retaliate against American planes based in Japan. Since U.S.-UN Commander MacArthur still maintained that the Chinese did not pose a serious threat to his forces, he began a new offensive against the North Koreans in the hope of ending the war by Christmas. Then, on November 25, the U.S. and UN troops unexpectedly found themselves facing masses of experienced Chinese soldiers numbering in the hundreds of thousands. For some time, the soldiers had been moving into North Korea under the cover of night, virtually undetected. The MacArthur offensive rapidly turned into a rout, with casualties mounting to approximately 13,000[7] as the U.S.-UN troops were pushed back across the 38th parallel and the Chinese recaptured Pyongyang.

One military defeat followed another, causing the President himself to come under fire, not from the enemy but from his critics. Conservative Republicans, including members of the China Lobby, demanded that the Korean conflict be widened to include mainland China. Others, like the British government, recommended that the administration cut its losses and negotiate a cease-fire. Truman contributed to his own problems by admitting at a press conference that he was thinking about using atomic bombs as a last, desperate resort. He told reporters that the United States was prepared to take "whatever steps are necessary to meet the military situation, just as we always have. That includes every weapon we have."[8] Of course, the headlines that followed made it even harder for him to stay within the confines of the limited war that he had set.

The Korean War turned into a disaster for the United States and its UN allies once the Chinese crossed the 38th parallel on December 31. The invading forces soon managed to take Seoul, but the farther south the Chinese moved, the more difficult it became for them to maintain their supply lines. As a result, U.S.-UN forces were gradually able to mount a counteroffensive and reclaim the territory they had lost. By March, they had taken back Seoul and soon approached the 38th parallel once again. At this point, the Truman administration and the allied governments thought the time had come to negotiate a cease-fire to end the war. They were willing to abandon plans to reunify Korea; however, they did not anticipate General MacArthur's reaction.

While President Truman was directing the actual conflict in Korea, he was also waging another military battle— a battle with Douglas MacArthur. Because the popular general had difficulty adjusting to the concept of limited war, he caused numerous problems for his civilian commander in chief. MacArthur had released a number of public statements urging that the war be widened. He undermined Truman's efforts to neutralize Formosa during the Korean conflict by paying a personal visit to Chiang Kai-shek on his island fortress and telling the press that he supported the Nationalists' desires to reclaim mainland China. As early as August 1950, a month before the perilous Inchon landing, Truman sent senior diplomat W. Averell Harriman to talk with the general and remind him that, as a military officer, he was obliged to carry out the President's policies. MacArthur agreed to heed Harriman's counsel, but before the end of the month, he issued another statement backing Chiang and the Nationalists' determination to regain control of mainland China. An irate Truman asked Secretary of Defense Louis Johnson to have the general retract the statement, but Johnson refused. Rebuffed by the difficult and quarrelsome Johnson for the last time, Truman asked George Marshall to return to government service and become his new secretary of defense.

Seeming determined to make himself the leading spokesman for the China Lobby and the President's other conservative critics in Congress, General MacArthur persisted in his disastrous course. In mid-October, Harry Truman flew to Wake Island in the Pacific to meet with the outspoken, uncooperative general. He wanted to make sure that MacArthur fully understood how important it was to keep the war in Korea limited and to personally receive the general's pledge to make no more comments about Chiang to reporters. The President was also curious to see for himself the man whom many regarded as one of the nation's outstanding military figures. At their meeting, the general apologized for embarrassing the Truman administration with his press releases and promised to stay out of politics.

The President thought he had accomplished his mission, that he had silenced MacArthur. However, his troubles with the general were only beginning. When the Chinese began to inflict heavy losses on U.S.-UN forces, the general made known to all who would listen his dissatisfaction with fighting a limited war. After the President refused to give him permission to bomb Chinese bases and supply lines, MacArthur retaliated by giving interviews accusing the administration of hurting the war effort and publicly criticizing the orders that restrained him. Conservative Republicans in Congress quickly took up MacArthur's cause, which led Truman to notify all overseas officers that their statements would have to be cleared in Washington before being released to the public.

Because he believed in keeping his commanders informed of policy decisions affecting them, Truman sent MacArthur rough drafts of the cease-fire plan he was preparing once the war finally stabilized along the 38th parallel. MacArthur, however, took matters into his own hands. Without consulting Washington, he offered to negotiate with the enemy commander in the field and threatened to attack China by air and sea if the offer was not accepted. An expert on Asia, MacArthur knew that the wording of his statement would antagonize and humiliate the Chinese. Truman recorded his reaction: "This was a most extraordinary statement for a military commander of the United Nations to issue on his own responsibility. It was an act totally disregarding all directives to abstain from any declarations of foreign policy. It was in open defiance of my orders as President and as Commander in Chief. This was a challenge to the authority of the President under the Constitution. It also flouted the policy of the United Nations."[9] The President was furious. He wanted to remove MacArthur from his post right away, but realized that he had to bide his time. As a politician, the President knew that if he fired MacArthur at once, he would cause an uproar in Congress just when the legislators were about to consider funding for the Marshall Plan and NATO, two important measures that needed bipartisan support.

General MacArthur used his reprieve to launch another attack on Truman's foreign policy. When Representative Joseph Martin, the Republican minority leader, wrote to the general asking him to comment on the war, MacArthur replied with an impassioned letter. Objecting to the restraints imposed by fighting a limited war, he wrote a spirited defense of his actions, expressed his opposition to the cease-fire, and concluded with the warning, "There is no substitute for victory."[10] On April 5, Congressman Martin set off a furor when he read the correspondence to members of the House of Representatives. The White House was besieged with so many letters and telegrams condemning the President that Truman knew he had to take action. The former World War I captain of Battery D promptly fired his five-star World War II general.

Despite all that had passed between them, Harry Truman respected the distinguished general for his long service in the army, his inspired leadership in World War II, and his successful management of occupied Japan. Therefore, as a courtesy to MacArthur, the President tried to have the orders relieving him of command hand-delivered to the general so that he could read them in private and prepare a response to the formal public announcement. When the necessary arrangements could not be made, however, the President chose to move swiftly lest the general learn about his pending dismissal through unofficial channels and decide to resign first. So on April 11, 1951, the President informed White House reporters that he was removing MacArthur from his post and would assign General Matthew B. Ridgway to replace him.

Just as Truman had expected, his decision to fire MacArthur was immensely unpopular. Conservative Republicans in Congress denounced him for relieving the general and took him to task for his policies in Asia, while

Gallup polls revealed that public opinion favored the general over the president 69 to 29.[11] Upon his return to Washington, MacArthur received a hero's welcome and delivered an emotional farewell address to Congress, lamenting that old soldiers don't die, "they just fade away."[12] MacArthur, however, didn't fade away all at once. Instead, the general testified before a Senate committee investigating his dismissal. He lambasted the administration for refusing to take his advice on the conduct of the war and self-righteously denied that he had made any mistakes. During the seven-week-long hearings, Defense Secretary Marshall and other members of the Truman administration successfully rebutted MacArthur's claim that they had supported his views on the Korean conflict. The senators did not vindicate the general. In the end, MacArthur retired to a suite at the Waldorf Towers in New York City and gradually withdrew from politics.

Truman had known that the public's emotional outbursts were short-lived and that current heroes were soon forgotten. In the Senate, MacArthur's supporters were quite willing to approve the administration's peace treaty with Japan, ending American occupation of the defeated nation. The prospects for international cooperation also improved once the general was removed from the scene. The Soviets and the Chinese approached Truman to start negotiations for a truce in Korea, and a "Little Armistice" was achieved in November 1951. However, each side continued to probe the other's defenses so that the conflict dragged on until July 1953, long after Truman had left office. By the time the Korean War finally ended, approximately 33,600 members of the American armed services had been killed, 103,300 were wounded, and another 5,100 were missing or captured.[13]

The Korean War taught Harry Truman and the people he led what it meant to fight a limited war in the nuclear age. Lacking historical guidelines, the President had made up the rules as he went along, just as he had had to accept the consequences of abandoning his originally modest aims for more grandiose ones. Not everyone shared his goals, nor did everyone approve of the means he chose. As a result, the President had to resist both the pressure to pursue victory at any price and the equally strong pressure to seek peace at any price. He met with formidable opposition when he decided not to extend the war to other Asian countries and not to use atomic weapons. Nevertheless, he succeeded in showing the world that communist expansion could be contained. In 1952, with the war at a standstill, the President faced new decisions and new challenges. The public waited to hear if he would choose to run for office yet again.

NINE

THE LATER YEARS

On March 29, 1952, the nation's most powerful and respected Democrats gathered in the Washington Armory for the party's annual Jefferson-Jackson Day dinner. Dressed in tuxedos and elegant gowns, they sat at gaily decorated tables, eating, drinking, and exchanging gossip. President Truman and Bess, accompanied by Secretary of State Acheson and his wife, Alice, were seated on a platform with several other Democratic notables. As the featured after-dinner speaker, Truman would deliver a rousing partisan talk, praising the accomplishments of the Democratic party. The Democrats in the armory that night had reason to be proud of the President's fine record of achievements over the past seven years and were ready to cheer him on as he spoke.

When dessert and coffee had finally been served, the President stood up and gave the speech his enthusiastic audience had been waiting to hear. When he came to the last paragraph, delight quickly turned to dismay as the assembled party members heard him say, "I shall not be a candidate for reelection. I have served my country long, and I think efficiently and honestly. I shall not accept renomination. I do not feel that it is my duty to spend another four years in the White House."[1] His unexpected announcement surprised and shocked everyone in the room—everyone, that is, except Bess Truman, who had known it was coming and rejoiced. Although she would have been willing to endure another four years in the White House if she'd had to, she yearned for the privacy of her home on North Delaware Street.

Truman could have run again; he was exempt from provisions of the Twenty-second Amendment to the Constitution, passed in 1951, which limited Presidents to two terms of office. He knew how Bess felt, however, and he thought it was time for someone else to take over the responsibilities of the nation's highest office. In 1950 he had written a personal memo explaining, "In my opinion eight years as President is enough and sometimes too much for any man to serve in this capacity. There is a lure in power. It can get into a man's blood just as gambling and lust for money have been known to do."[2] He was concerned about one man staying in power too long. If this were to happen, Truman felt that the president would lose touch with the public's needs and interests. From his study of history he had concluded that for a democratic government to truly reflect the wishes of the people, it was necessary to change leaders frequently.

Before Harry Truman could retire from the presidency, he still had to deal with the many important national and political matters that came across his desk. On that desk was a sign, "The buck stops here," Truman's way of reminding those who came in to see him that *he* made the decisions and that *he* was responsible for running the government. A threatened steelworkers' strike was one of the crucial issues that demanded his immediate attention, since steel was used in the tanks and other military equipment needed by American troops fighting in Korea. At first, when the unions and management were not able to reach an agreement on pay and working conditions, President Truman referred their dispute to the Wage Stabilization Board, which gave them ninety-nine days to settle their differences. He did not use negotiators provided by the Taft-Hartley Act because the act gave them only eighty days to work out a compromise, and the armed services needed those extra nineteen days of steel production. The board reported that management wanted to increase the price of steel to $12.00 a ton to offset the cost of the 26-cent hourly wage increase demanded by the workers. Truman rejected management's proposal as inflationary, reasoning that if the price of steel went up, steel products such as autos and refrigerators would become more costly. When further negotiations became deadlocked, the steelworkers again threatened to strike.

On April 8, 1952, as the strike date approached, President Truman issued an order seizing the nation's steel mills in order to keep them in operation. The mill owners brought a lawsuit, which soon reached the Supreme Court. In June the justices decided that the President lacked the emergency power to take over the mills, reasoning that Korea was a police action and not a formally declared war. When the government returned the mills to their owners, the workers promptly went out on a strike that lasted for fifty-three days, the longest steel strike in American history. Moreover, the President's fears were realized when some American forces in Korea ran short of ammunition during the work stoppage. In the end, the workers got an increase of 21 cents an hour, and the price of steel went up by $5.20 a ton.[3]

Right after the Supreme Court's decision, Congress had rejected Harry Truman's request for a law giving the President the right to seize strikebound plants vital to the national defense. Truman then lost another battle to Congress over the McCarran-Walter Immigration Act, which went into effect on December 24, 1952, after Congress had overridden the President's veto. Truman labeled the law "an inhumane policy"[4] because it denied people from Asia and southeastern Europe entry to the United States, and allowed admittance to only 156,000 immigrants a year. The act remained in force until 1965, when Congress adopted a less restrictive policy toward people seeking to enter the United States.

Although he had announced that he would not seek

another term of office, Harry Truman became deeply involved in presidential politics, helping his party find a wor-
thy candidate for the 1952 election. He felt that his Vice
President, Alben Barkley, was too old to serve, and after
Supreme Court Chief Justice Fred Vinson turned him down
he finally suggested Governor Adlai E. Stevenson of Illinois, a choice the Democratic National Convention eagerly
accepted, but one that Truman came to regret. Truman
was a decisive man who relished action and enjoyed the
rough-and-tumble of American politics, while the Illinois
governor wavered back and forth before finally agreeing
to be his party's standard-bearer. At times Stevenson
seemed unwilling to make the effort needed to win the
nation's highest office, an attitude that disturbed the President. Ever a Democratic partisan, Truman was even more
troubled when Dwight D. Eisenhower accepted the Republican nomination for the presidency. A very popular leader,
Eisenhower had served as president of Columbia University from 1948 to 1950, until President Truman appointed
him postwar supreme allied commander of NATO forces
in Europe.

From the President's point of view, the campaign was
very disappointing. Faced with Republican charges that
the Truman administration was scandalously corrupt and
sympathetic to communists, Stevenson flatly refused to
run on the Democratic record of the past seven years.
Truman could not tolerate the attack on his reputation and
achievements, for he was too much of a fighter to sit back
and play the role of an impartial observer about to retire.
He insisted on defending his record and his party's honor,
so in late September, accompanied by Margaret, he went
out on a whistle-stop tour to refute the Republicans' accusations. Despite his efforts, the November election was a
fiasco for Adlai Stevenson, with Eisenhower easily winning
the presidency by a margin of more than 6 million popular
votes and 353 electoral votes. At first, President Truman
was very upset with the election returns, but Bess helped

him to take a longer view of the situation. He came to realize that the Democrats had been defeated before and would bounce back again.

About three weeks after the election, Truman became concerned with a more immediate personal matter. The health of his ninety-year-old mother-in-law, Madge Wallace, who had suffered a stroke, started to decline. On December 5, after a bout with pneumonia, she died in the White House, across the hall from the President's study. Mrs. Wallace had moved in with the Trumans when they first settled in Washington and had lived with them on and off ever since, and the Trumans still shared her home in Independence. Even after her son-in-law became President of the United States, she had continued to find fault with him, and in 1948, she had even wondered aloud why he was running against "that nice man, Thomas E. Dewey."[5] Truman did not complain, however, and continued to treat her with respect until the day she died. To protect his grieving wife from unwanted publicity, he arranged for Bess's mother to receive a private service and burial in Independence.

As his presidency drew to a close, Harry Truman focused his attention on the needs of the incoming administration. Traditionally, when the opposing party's presidential candidate won the election, the outgoing president did little to ease the burden his successor faced. Truman, however, realized that the United States, now a major world power, could ill afford a disorganized and confusing transition from one president to the next. He also remembered how difficult it had been for him to learn all he needed to know when he suddenly took office. For these reasons he was determined to find a way to introduce the new president to the responsibilities of government and establish an orderly transfer of power. Even while the campaign was under way, the President arranged to keep both candidates informed about current developments on the international scene. Then, on November 18, once Eisenhower became president-elect, Truman held a twenty-minute private meeting with him in the Oval Office to discuss the practical problems of being chief executive and ways to make the transition as smooth as possible. Afterward, some of Truman's cabinet officials briefed Eisenhower and his aides on the continuing foreign policy problems the new administration would have to handle.

As Inauguration Day approached, the Trumans gave a series of farewell parties for members of the cabinet and the White House staff. A visit from Winston Churchill also livened the family's last weeks in the White House. Then, as Eisenhower prepared to take the oath of office, he decided to disregard time-honored presidential rituals and declined the Trumans' invitation to come to the White House for a preinaugural lunch. He also announced that he would wear a homburg rather than the traditional top hat for the swearing-in ceremony, so Truman abandoned the top hat as well. In another breach of courtesy, the president-elect suggested that Harry Truman call for him en route to the inauguration. However, Harry Truman was still President and insisted that Eisenhower meet him at the White House, as was the custom. Eisenhower reluctantly agreed, but unlike previous presidents, he refused to step out of his car until the Trumans arrived. Whether for partisan or personal reasons, Eisenhower had certainly demonstrated his dislike for the outgoing President, and after the slights Truman had received, the feeling became mutual.

On January 20, 1953, once the formal ceremonies were completed, a White House limousine took the Trumans to Dean Acheson's house for a private luncheon with former members of the Truman cabinet. Over the years, the professional relationship between the feisty self-educated President and his polished, aristocratic secretary of state had turned into a genuine friendship. On the ride over to the Achesons', Margaret Truman turned to her father and teased, "Hello, *Mr.* Truman." He laughed heartily at her joke.[6] Throughout Margaret's life, her father had been called by honorary titles—Judge, Senator, Mr. President—but now, for the first time that she could remember, he was out of office. To the Trumans' surprise, a crowd of about 500 well-wishers greeted them outside the Achesons' home.

Later, when they arrived at the train station, they were even more astonished to find over 5,000 people waiting to see them off on their trip to Independence. Harry Truman was so touched by this tribute that he stood on the rear platform of the train and told them: "This is the first time you have sent me home in a blaze of glory. I can't adequately express my appreciation for what you are doing. I'll never forget it if I live to be a hundred. And that's just what I expect to do!"[7] Not to be outdone by the citizens of Washington, D.C., approximately 10,000 Missourians gathered at the train station in Kansas City to celebrate the Trumans' return to their home state, and some 1,500 more people waited in Independence to welcome them back to 219 North Delaware Street.

When the family finally arrived home, the former president calmly took the family baggage upstairs to the attic for storage. However, the Trumans could not simply resume their normal routines, because a grateful public was not ready to let them live in privacy. It was impossible for the former president to walk down the street, get a haircut, or shop without being stopped and greeted by strangers. Autograph seekers made it difficult for him to join old friends for lunch at a restaurant. Since he did not want to dine alone in his office, he eventually accepted an invitation to become a member of the Kansas City Club, a private club frequented by local Republicans. There, over a quiet meal, he learned how quickly old political feuds could be forgotten. He also faced a more personal problem in adjusting to life as an ordinary citizen; he missed the challenges, the pressure, and the decision-making of the presidency. As he explained to a reporter, "I still don't feel like a completely private citizen and I don't suppose I ever will. It's still almost impossible to do as other people do, even though I've tried. You can't always be as you want to be after you've been under those bright lights."[8]

During his first months out of office, he had to cope with the arrival of more than 70,000 pieces of mail, even though he was not supplied with secretarial help from the government, as later ex-presidents would be. Nor were former presidents guarded by the Secret Service in those days. To their great disappointment, the Trumans found that they had to keep the iron fence that had been installed around their property when he was chief executive. While the family initially thought it imprisoned them, they soon began to value the protection it gave them from countless souvenir hunters and curiosity seekers. Although the town of Independence did provide Truman with a bodyguard, Mike Westwood, in 1961, it wasn't until the assassination of John F. Kennedy in 1963 that Secret Service agents were assigned to protect former presidents.

Harry Truman left office as he had entered it—without a large personal fortune to see him through the years that lay ahead. He rejected many important job offers and endorsements that would have guaranteed him financial security for the rest of his life because he did not want to use the president's prestige for personal gain. Instead, he went to work as a writer, preparing a column for a syndicated newspaper chain and recalling events from the past for his autobiography, two volumes of reminiscences, published in 1955 and 1956. In 1958 his financial situation improved when he, Vivian, and Mary Jane Truman accepted an offer from developers who wanted to buy the Grandview farm and turn it into a shopping center. Proceeds from that sale guaranteed that they would all be able to live in comfort for the rest of their days.

Although Harry Truman had originally intended to erect a library to house his presidential and personal papers on a portion of the Grandview acreage, he was able to sell his share of the farm without regret. To his delight, the town of Independence had already set aside some land for the library in a local park just a mile from North Delaware Street, a site much more accessible to the public. To raise funds for the Truman library, the former president went on exhausting speaking tours in addition to his other activities, and as a result, the building was dedicated in 1957. Working at an office in the library, acknowledging contributions, collecting more documents, and greeting visitors kept Truman busy. Now he had a purpose in life that he had been missing: he could use the library to educate the American people about their nation's past and his own contributions to its history. In 1961 he even agreed to be filmed for a television series about the presidency and to record an oral history. Of course, he also enjoyed escorting his successors on tours of the Truman Library, but perhaps the visit that pleased Harry Truman the most was the one President Lyndon Johnson made in 1965, when he signed the Medicare Bill into law in Truman's presence. Although Medicare was aimed at providing medical insurance for elderly people, it was a fitting tribute to Truman's attempts to secure health coverage for all Americans, a concern that has continued into the 1990s.

While Harry Truman had retired from public office, he did not withdraw entirely from the political scene. In 1953, when Republicans repeated their charges that his administration had been riddled with communists, he gave a radio speech vigorously defending his record, and with great indignation he refused to testify before the House Committee on Un-American Activities concerning those charges. Not only did he defend the past, he also looked ahead to the future. As a lifelong Democrat, he wanted his party to pick the best-qualified presidential candidates available, and he made his preferences known. Since he could never resist a political fight, he continued to campaign for the Democratic ticket even when he did not entirely approve of his party's choices. At the 1956 Democratic National Convention, Truman tried unsuccessfully to have Averell Harriman, a recent governor of New York, replace

Adlai Stevenson as the party's presidential candidate, but the Illinois governor was renominated and lost once again to Eisenhower.

In 1959, Truman traveled to Washington to advise party leaders on possible candidates for the 1960 presidential elections, but they did not share his enthusiasm for Missouri Senator Stuart Symington. Truman felt that their choice, John F. Kennedy, was too young and that the American people were not yet ready to accept a Catholic president. Truman also advised Lyndon Johnson not to run as Kennedy's vice presidential candidate, but the Texas senator accepted the nomination just the same. By the time the campaign got under way, Truman found himself making speeches in support of the Democratic ticket, and he enjoyed Kennedy's triumph over Republican candidate Richard M. Nixon. Truman was even more pleased by a dinner the Kennedys gave in 1961 at the White House for the former president and members of his administration. He was so gratified to be invited back to the White House after an eight-year absence that Truman even gave an impromptu piano performance before the assembled guests. Two years later, the Kennedy assassination upset Truman so much that he could not face reporters to answer their questions as he usually did.

While working at the Truman Library and politicking gave the former president much personal satisfaction, he also took pleasure in activities and events he could share with his wife. Back in March 1953 the Trumans had accepted an invitation to visit Hawaii, where they had enjoyed a relaxing vacation. In June of the same year they started out on a leisurely auto trip to Washington, but the crowds they attracted soon turned their journey into another whistle-stop tour, and for the sake of privacy, they chose to use other means of transportation in the future. They traveled to Europe twice, once in 1956, when they managed to include a visit to Winston Churchill, and again in 1958. Then, in 1962, Harry Truman returned abroad to represent the United States at the funeral of King Paul of

Greece. The Trumans rejoiced when Margaret married Clifton Daniel, an editor for the *New York Times*, in April 1956 at the same church in Independence where Harry and Bess had been married thirty-seven years earlier. In the years to come, the Daniels presented the elderly couple with four grandsons. While the former president enjoyed reading to the children and telling them stories, he was not a physically active grandfather.

Unfortunately, like many older couples the Trumans gradually found their circle of relatives and friends diminishing as death claimed the lives of Vivian Truman, Ethel and Nellie Noland, Jim Pendergast, George Marshall, Winston Churchill, and Dean Acheson, among others. Illness also took a toll on the former president and his wife. In 1954, at age seventy, Harry Truman suffered a severe gallbladder attack. At the time he was waiting to go on stage, to play himself in a local production of Irving Berlin's show, *Call Me Madam*. The musical comedy gently poked fun at a fictitious diplomat—modeled on Bess's friend Pearl Mesta, onetime ambassador to Luxembourg—who was supposedly appointed by President Truman to serve in an imaginary European kingdom. Instead of enjoying a brief walk-on role, Truman was rushed to the hospital, where his gallbladder was quickly removed. He came through the procedure without difficulty but suffered an allergic reaction to the antibiotic the doctors had used and took longer to recover than he would have liked. In 1959 it was Bess's turn to have surgery, which successfully rid her of a large noncancerous tumor.

As Truman entered his eighties, his health worsened. In 1964 he fell in the bathroom, cracking two ribs, but after he was released from the hospital he still continued his morning walks. As time went on, however, he became quite frail, and by 1967 he could no longer go to the library. By the time he reached the age of eighty-eight, his joints were so swollen and stiff from arthritis that he even had trouble climbing the stairs. Toward the end of the year, he was admitted to the hospital with heart and lung problems. The doctors could not help him, and he gradually slipped into a coma. On December 26, 1972, he died. After turning down offers of a state funeral for the late president, Bess and Margaret invited Harry Truman's famous associates as well as the ordinary people he cared about to attend a simple service in the auditorium of the Truman Library. He is buried in the library courtyard.

Most people agree that Harry Truman was a president who made decisions and got things done, and that is how he would probably wish to be remembered. Writing about past presidents in his memoirs, he discussed the stresses and strains of office and the need to be independent and decisive. He could easily have been writing about himself when he wrote: "A president cannot always be popular. He has to be able to say yes and no, and more often no to most of the propositions that are put up to him by partisan groups and special interests who are always pulling at the White House for one thing or another. If a President is easily influenced . . . he is a complete washout. Every great President in our history had a policy of his own, which eventually won the people's support."[9]

Whether or not Harry Truman should be ranked among the greatest American presidents is still subject to debate. In a 1983 survey, 970 professional historians rated Abraham Lincoln, George Washington, and Franklin Roosevelt as the three most outstanding presidents of the United States. Andrew Jackson, Thomas Jefferson, Theodore Roosevelt, and Woodrow Wilson tied for fourth place. However, in the same year, when a Gallup poll asked the American people, "Of all the presidents we have ever had, who do you wish were President today?" the public placed only John Kennedy and Franklin Roosevelt ahead of Truman. A 1975 public opinion poll had previously ranked Truman fourth on a list of America's greatest presidents.[10] Truman had always put his faith in the American people, and they did not fail him.

SOURCE NOTES

CHAPTER ONE

1. Margaret Truman, ed., *Where the Buck Stops: The Personal and Private Writings of Harry S. Truman* (New York: Warner Books, 1989), p. 371.

2. Ibid., p. 372.

3. Merle Miller, *Plain Speaking: An Oral Biography of Harry S. Truman* (New York: Berkley Books, 1974), p. 214.

4. Ibid., p. 19.

5. Margaret Truman, *Harry S. Truman* (New York: William Morrow, 1973), p. 58.

6. Margaret Truman, *Bess W. Truman* (New York: Jove Books, 1987), p. 72.

7. Merle Miller, p. 100.

8. David McCullough, *Truman* (New York: Simon & Schuster, 1992), p. 138.

CHAPTER TWO

1. David McCullough, *Truman* (New York: Simon & Schuster, 1992), p. 157.

2. Merle Miller, *Plain Speaking: An Oral Biography of Harry S. Truman* (New York: Berkley Books, 1974), p. 126.

3. Joseph Gies, *Harry S. Truman: A Pictorial Biography* (New York: Doubleday, 1968), p. 16.

4. Ibid.

5. Merle Miller, p. 134.

6. McCullough, p. 189.

7. Ibid., p. 187.

8. Harry S. Truman, "Years of Decisions," *Memoirs*, 2 vols. (New York: Doubleday, 1956), vol. 1., p. 144.

9. Ibid.
10. Ibid., p. 161.
11. McCullough, p 247.
12. Truman, p. 193.
13. Margaret Truman, *Harry S. Truman* (New York: William Morrow, 1973), p. 183.
14. Harry Truman, p. 19.

CHAPTER THREE

1. Margaret Truman, *Harry S. Truman* (New York: William Morrow, 1973), p. 242.
2. David McCullough, *Truman* (New York: Simon & Schuster, 1992), p. 356.
3. Margaret Truman, p. 304.
4. Ibid., pp. 229–30.
5. Robert Donovan, *Crisis and Conflict: The Presidency of Harry S. Truman, 1945–1948* (New York: Norton, 1977), 165.
6. Margaret Truman, p. 246.
7. Margaret Truman, *Bess W. Truman* (New York: Jove Books, 1987), pp. 301–2.
8. Merle Miller, *Plain Speaking: An Oral Biography of Harry S. Truman* (New York: Berkley Books, 1974), p. 398.

CHAPTER FOUR

1. Richard Rhodes, *The Making of the Atomic Bomb* (New York: Simon & Schuster, 1986), p. 688.
2. David McCullough, *Truman* (New York: Simon & Schuster, 1992), p. 441.
3. John Keegan, *The Second World War* (New York: Penguin Books, 1990), p. 566.
4. Ibid., p. 568.
5. McCullough, p. 444.
6. Harry S. Truman, *Memoirs*, 2 vols. (New York: Doubleday, 1956), vol. 1., "Years of Decisions," p. 420.
7. Rhodes, p. 692.
8. Karl Taylor Compton, "If the Atomic Bomb Had Not Been Used," *The Atlantic Monthly*, December 1946, pp. 54–56, reprinted in Edward Fogelman, ed., *Hiroshima: The Decision to Use the A-Bomb* (New York: Scribner's, 1964), p. 92.
9. Robert Donovan, *Conflict and Crisis: The Presidency of Harry S. Truman, 1945–1948* (New York: Norton, 1977), p. 96.
10. Compton, p. 92.
11. Donovan, pp. 96–97.
12. Robert C. Batchelder, "Dropping the Atomic Bomb: Right

or Wrong?" *The Irreversible Decision 1939–1950* (Boston: Houghton Mifflin, 1961), pp. 111–12, reprinted in Edward Fogelman, ed., *Hiroshima: The Decision to Use the A-Bomb* (New York: Scribner's, 1964), pp. 106–12.

13. Harry Truman, p. 2.

14. Margaret Truman, *Harry S. Truman* (New York: William Morrow, 1973), p. 332.

15. Donovan, p. 308.

CHAPTER FIVE

1. Robert Donovan, *Crisis and Conflict: The Presidency of Harry S. Truman, 1945–1948* (New York: Norton, 1977), p. 215.

2. Ibid.

3. Clark Clifford, *Counsel to the President: A Memoir* (New York: Random House, 1991), p. 91.

4. Ibid., p. 93.

5. Donovan, p. 242.

6. Ibid., p. 108.

7. Margaret Truman, *Harry S. Truman* (New York: William Morrow, 1973), p. 351.

8. Donovan, p. 113.

9. Ibid., p. 128.

10. Richard Hofstadter, William Miller, Daniel Aaron, Winthrop Jordan, and Leon F. Litwack, *The United States* (Englewood Cliffs, N.J.: Prentice-Hall, 1979), p. 374.

11. Harry S. Truman, *Memoirs*, 2 vols. (New York: Doubleday, 1956), vol. 1., "Years of Decisions," p. 180.

12. Donovan, pp. 147–48.

13. Harry Truman, p. 180.

14. Merle Miller, *Plain Speaking: An Oral Biography of Harry S. Truman* (New York: Berkley Books, 1974), p. 163.

CHAPTER SIX

1. Clark Clifford, *Counsel to the President* (New York: Random House, 1991), p. 105.

2. Robert Donovan, *Crisis and Conflict: The Presidency of Harry S. Truman, 1945–1948* (New York: Norton, 1977), p. 191.

3. Harry S. Truman, *Memoirs*, 2 vols. (New York: Doubleday, 1956), vol. 2., "Years of Trial and Hope," p. 102.

4. Dean Acheson, *Present at the Creation: My Years in the State Department* (New York: Norton, 1969), p. 222.

5. Eric F. Goldman, *The Crucial Decade: America, 1945–1955* (New York: Knopf, 1956), p. 60.

6. Donovan, p. 376.

7. Clifford, p. 13.

8. Merle Miller, *Plain Speaking: An Oral Biography of Harry S. Truman* (New York: Berkley Books, 1974), pp. 257–58.

9. Harry Truman, p. 110.

10. Acheson, p. 233.

11. Richard Hofstadter, William Miller, Daniel Aaron, Winthrop Jordan, and Leon F. Litwack, *The United States* (Englewood Cliffs, N.J.: Prentice-Hall, 1979), p. 379.

12. Harry Truman, p. 124.

13. Ibid., p. 130.

14. Ibid., p. 131.

CHAPTER SEVEN

1. Harry S. Truman, *Memoirs*, 2 vols. (New York: Doubleday, 1956), vol. 2., "Years of Trial and Hope," p. 221.

2. Joseph Gies, *Harry S. Truman: A Pictorial Biography* (New York: Doubleday, 1968), p. 99.

3. Harry Truman, p. 179.

4. Gies, p. 102.

5. Ibid., p. 108.

6. Margaret Truman, *Harry S. Truman* (New York: William Morrow, 1973), p. 123.

7. Ibid., p. 22.

8. Harry Truman, p. 219.

9. Gies, p. 84.

10. Harry Truman, p. 224.

11. David McCullough, *Truman* (New York: Simon & Schuster, 1992), p. 723.

12. Dean Acheson, *Present at the Creation: My Years in the State Department* (New York: Norton, 1969), p. 264.

13. Harry Truman, p. 236.

14. Ibid., p. 237.

15. Ibid., p. 275.

16. McCullough, p. 768.

17. Harry Truman, p. 270.

18. Ibid., p. 284.

19. Ibid.

20. McCullough, p. 829.

21. Margaret Truman, p. 503.

22. Ibid., p. 488.

CHAPTER EIGHT

1. Joseph Gies, *Harry S. Truman: A Pictorial Biography* (New York: Doubleday, 1968), p. 134.

2. Harry Truman, *Memoirs*, 2 vols. (New York: Doubleday, 1956), vol. 2., "Years of Trial and Hope," p. 333.

3. Dean Acheson, *Present at the Creation: My Years in the State Department* (New York: Norton, 1969), p. 147.

4. Gies, p. 165.

5. Harry Truman, p. 371.

6. Richard Hofstadter, William Miller, Daniel Aaron, Winthrop Jordan, and Leon F. Litwack, *The United States* (Englewood Cliffs, N.J.: Prentice-Hall, 1979), p. 382.

7. Margaret Truman, *Harry S. Truman* (New York: William Morrow, 1973), p. 494.

8. McCullough, p. 821.

9. Ibid., p. 837.

10. Acheson, p. 520.

11. Margaret Truman, p. 516.

12. Ibid., p. 517.

13. Acheson, p. 652.

CHAPTER NINE

1. Margaret Truman, *Bess W. Truman* (New York: Jove Books, 1987), p. 441.

2. Harry Truman, *Memoirs*, 2 vols. (New York: Doubleday, 1956), vol. 2, "Years of Trial and Hope," p. 488.

3. David McCullough, *Truman* (New York: Simon & Schuster, 1992), p. 902.

4. Margaret Truman, p. 479.

5. Miller, p. 109.

6. Margaret Truman, *Harry S. Truman* (New York: William Morrow, 1973), p. 558.

7. Ibid.

8. McCullough, p. 929.

9. Harry Truman, p. 196.

10. All survey data in this paragraph can be found in James MacGregor Burns, J. W. Peltason, and Thomas E. Cronin, *Government by the People*, 13th alt. ed. (Englewood Cliffs, N.J.: Prentice Hall, 1989), p. 315.

GLOSSARY

Cabinet The heads of government departments who advise the President.

De facto recognition: According to international law, accepting that a state exists without passing judgment on the way it originated. De facto recognition does not require an exchange of ambassadors.

De jure recognition: According to international law, acknowledging that a state gained control of its territory through legitimate means and is a valued member of the international community. De jure recognition requires an exchange of ambassadors.

Demagogue: A person who inflames public opinion for his or her own advantage by distorting events or damaging the reputations of others.

Demobilization: The process of returning the armed forces to civilian life.

Inflation: A cycle of rising prices.

Injunction: A court order to stop doing something.

Jurisdictional strikes: Strikes over which union is supposed to perform a given task.

Minimum wage: The lowest legal hourly pay unskilled workers can receive.

Political patronage: Appointing loyal party supporters to government jobs.

Precedence: Rules concerning who goes first.

Protocol: Rules of etiquette and proper manners.

Reconversion: Switching from a wartime to a peacetime economy.

BIBLIOGRAPHY

Acheson, Dean. *Present at the Creation: My Years in the State Department*. New York: Norton, 1969.

Clifford, Clark. *Counsel to the President*. New York: Random House, 1991.

Donovan, Robert. *Conflict and Crisis: The Presidency of Harry S. Truman, 1945–1948*. New York: Norton, 1977.

Fogelman, Edward, ed., *Hiroshima: The Decision to Use the A-Bomb*. New York: Scribner's, 1964.

Gies, Joseph. *Harry S. Truman: A Pictorial Biography*. New York: Doubleday, 1968.

Goldman, Eric. *The Crucial Decade: America, 1945–1955*. New York: Knopf, 1956.

Hofstadter, Richard, and others. *The United States*. Englewood Cliffs, N.J.: Prentice-Hall, 1979, pp. 367–88.

Keegan, John. *The Second World War*. New York: Penguin Books, 1990.

McCullough, David. *Truman*. New York: Simon & Schuster, 1992.

Miller, Merle. *Plain Speaking: An Oral Biography of Harry S. Truman*. New York: Berkley Books, 1974.

Rhodes, Richard. *The Making of the Atomic Bomb*. New York: Simon & Schuster, 1986.

Truman, Harry. *Memoirs*. 2 vols. New York: Doubleday, 1956.

———. *Where the Buck Stops*, ed. Margaret Truman. New York: Warner Books, 1989.

Truman, Margaret. *Bess W. Truman*. New York: Jove Books, 1987.

———. *Harry S. Truman*. New York: William Morrow, 1973.

INDEX